TASK READING

Evelyn Davies
Norman Whitney
Meredith Pike-Baky
Laurie Blass

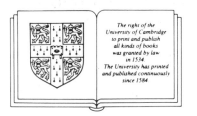

The right of the
University of Cambridge
to print and publish
all kinds of books
was granted by law
in 1534.
The University has printed
and published continuously
since 1584.

Cambridge University Press

Cambridge
New York   Port Chester
Melbourne   Sydney

Published by the Press Syndicate of the University of Cambridge
The Pitt Building, Trumpington Street, Cambridge CB2 1RP   UK
40 West 20th Street, New York, NY 10011   USA
10 Stamford Road, Oakleigh, Melbourne 3166, Australia

First published 1990
Second printing 1990

Printed in the United States of America

Library of Congress Cataloging-in-Publication Data
Task Reading / Evelyn Davies . . . [et al.].
    p.   cm.
    ISBN 0-521-35810-8
    1. English language — Textbooks for foreign speakers.   2. College
    readers. I. Davies, Evelyn
    PE1128.T328 1990
    428.6'4 — dc20   89-36653
                                                             CIP

British Library Cataloguing in Publication Data
Task Reading.
    1. English language. Comprehension
    I. Davies, Evelyn
    428.2

    ISBN 0-521-35810-8

Task Reading is an American English adaptation of the British English text, *Reasons
for Reading*, published by Heinemann Education Books Ltd., 1979.

Book, interior art, and cover designed on an electronic desktop publishing system
by M 'N O Production Services, Inc.

Contents

Introduction

Task Reading is intended for readers of English as a second language who have mastered some basic structures and vocabulary in English and who place into high-beginning to mid-intermediate classes. The purpose of the book is to help students recognize, read, understand, and enjoy a wide variety of reading selections in English; to help students apply to English the skills they already have in their first language; and to teach skills that will assist students in their other academic courses.

Task Reading has a storyline—one day in the life of two foreign students in the San Francisco Bay area. Their needs for reading in English provide the context for a variety of authentic reading tasks.

The book is set up in three parts:

1 Reading for Information
2 Reading for Meaning
3 Reading for Pleasure

Each part has five units, each of which is made up of four parts:

• Reading
• Practice
• Review
• Skills Check

Each part ends with a Reading Review.

The *Teacher's Notes* section at the back of the book presents an overview of how the book is organized, the goals of each chapter, and a general procedure for using the book. It includes unit-by-unit instructions to assist the teacher in making the most of this course.

Task Reading will help prepare the reader for the demands of reading English both in and out of the classroom. By working through this course, students will learn to recognize the purpose of these selections and thus will become better and more confident readers.

Reading for Information

1 PEOPLE

1 READING

A Read this **description**.

Machiko Morita is from Japan. She is a student. She has come to Bay View to study English. Machiko is twenty years old and single. She has dark brown eyes, long dark hair, and is 5'6" tall. She likes traveling, reading, and talking with friends. Machiko lives in Bay View with her friend Sue Brown. Their apartment is near Bay View Community College.

B Read this **form**.

macy's
Department Store

Employee Biography Form

NAME	Brown Susan
BIRTHDATE	4-29-70
SEX	F
MARITAL STATUS	single
ADDRESS	720 Bedford Drive
	Bay View Calif. 94888
TELEPHONE	(415) 555-8933
PRESENT TITLE	Salesperson (shoe dept.)
PERSON TO NOTIFY IN CASE OF EMERGENCY	Jane Brown 9 Lilac Ave. Woodbrae, CA (415)555-7301 Mother
	Susan Brown 5/15/—

C   Read this **letter**.

```
                                    Av. Atlântica, 343  apto. 201
                                    Rio de Janeiro, Brazil
                                    May 28, 19—


Director of Admissions
Bay View Community College
2995 Prospect Street
Bay View, California 94888

Dear Sir or Madam:

     I am interested in studying English at Bay View
Community College beginning next fall.  My sister
studied at your college before she went to the
university.  She liked it very much.
     I am twenty-one years old.  I am a Brazilian
citizen, and my native language is Portuguese.  I
have completed high school and have studied English
for six years.  I can understand English, but I need
practice speaking and writing.
     Do you have any special courses for business
English?  I would like to major in business.
     Please send me information about registration
dates, tuition fees, and dormitory rooms.  Thank you
very much.


                                    Sincerely,

                                    Roberto Costa
                                    Roberto Costa
```

2 PRACTICE

A   Find information about the following people.

MACHIKO   What country does Machiko come from?
            How old is she?
            How tall is she?
            What does she like to do in her free time?

SUE   Where does she work?

            What form did she fill out?

            How old is she?

            Is she married?

            What is her position?

ROBERTO   Why did Roberto write a letter?

            When does he want to come to Bay View?

            How did he learn about Bay View Community College?

            What is Roberto's nationality?

            What does he want to major in?

B   Write a description of Sue. Use the information from her Employee Biography Form on page 2. Use at least 60 words.

C   Complete this Student Record Card for Machiko. Use the information from the description of Machiko and from Sue Brown's (her roommate) employee form.

D   Make a Student Record Card like Machiko's and fill it out with information about yourself. Exchange these forms with a classmate and write a description of him or her. Then read your description to your classmate. What does your classmate think of it?

Student Record Card

Name _____

Address in U.S.A. _____

_____

Telephone _____ Age _____ Sex _____

Nationality _____ Native Language _____

Height _____ Hair Color _____ Eye Color _____

Occupation _____

Interests _____

E   Now fill in this Class Information Chart for each member of your class. Try to learn everyone's name as you are doing this.

Class Information Chart

Name (First) (Last)	Nationality	Hometown	Hobbies

3 REVIEW

Read these descriptions of students. Then complete the chart.

Toshi wants to improve his fluency in English. He spends his time meeting Americans and asking them questions. His major is engineering.

Heli likes all sports. She swims, plays tennis, and plays volleyball when she is not studying.

Maria's major is math. She is studying English and working as a teaching assistant in the math department.

Pierre is very interested in politics and history. His major is political science.

NAME	MAJOR	HOBBIES	COUNTRY	FIRST LANGUAGE
Heli	Physical education		Norway	
		music		Japanese
		soccer	France	
		photography	Mexico	Spanish

4 SKILLS CHECK

You have read	a description
	a form
	a letter

You have practiced	answering information questions
	writing a description
	filling in a chart

You have used these words and expressions:

biography	major
chart	marital status
description	nationality
employee	native language/country
form	registration
hobbies	title/position
letter	

2 PLACES

1 READING

It's Machiko's first day at Bay View Community College and she asks Sue how to get there.

MACHIKO: This is the address. How do I find it?

SUE: You need a Bay View **street map**. You can take this one.

MACHIKO: Where's Prospect Street?

SUE: You look in the **index**. See? Prospect is in square E-seven.

MACHIKO: I can't find it.

SUE: This is a **grid map**. First you find the letter *E* on the side. Then you find the number seven across the top. There it is!

MACHIKO: But how do I get *there* from *here*? Where is it in Bay View?

SUE: Let's look at the **scale of miles**. Prospect Street is about one mile from here.You can walk!

GRID MAP

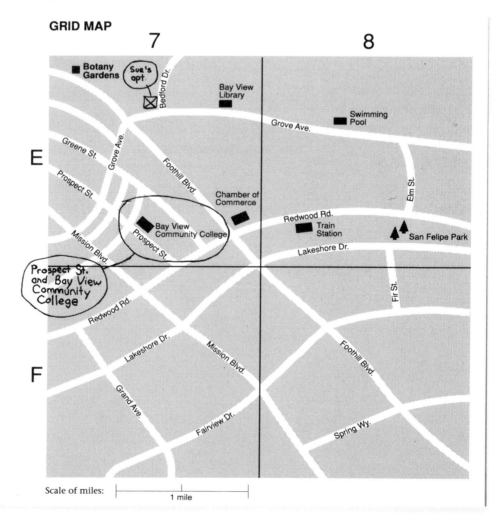

Scale of miles: |———|———| 1 mile

2 PRACTICE

A Look at the index below and find these streets. What square on a grid map would they be in?

Example: Cedar Avenue   _D-3_

    Cavendish Drive, West   _____

    Fielding Drive   _____

    Filbert Street   _____

    Oaktree Court   _____

    Ocean View Drive   _____

INDEX

Cavendish Dr. E. ··· C-10	Fern Wy. ··········· D-8	Oakridge Ct. ········ F-9
Cavendish Dr. W. ··· C-9	Fernwood Ct. ······· E-8	Oaktree Ct. ········ A-15
Cedar Ave. ·········· D-3	Fielding Dr.·········· G-9	Oakview Ave. ······· E-7
Celeste Ct. ········· A-12	Fiesta Pl. ··········· H-9	Oberlin Ave.········· D-3
Center St. ··········· C-8	Filbert St.··········· F-7	Ocean View Dr. ····· E-7
Central Ave.········· D-4	Finch Ct. ··········· J-7	O'Connell Ln. ·······L-12

KEY

Ave.	Avenue	**Pl.**	Place
Blvd.	Boulevard	**Rd .**	Road
Ct.	Court	**S.**	South
Dr.	Drive	**St.**	Street
E.	East	**W.**	West
Ln.	Lane	**Wy.**	Way
N.	North		

B Using the index and the key, tell a friend how to find other streets in Bay View. This key explains the abbreviations that are in the index.

Example: Where is O'Connell Lane?
        It's in square L-12.

C Find these grid locations on the grid map on page 6. Write the name of one street in each location.

Example: E-7 _Bedford Dr._

E-8 _____   F-7 _____

F-8 _____   E-7 _____

D Sue said, "Prospect Street is about one mile from here." Look at the grid map and the scale of miles and answer these questions.

    How far is it from the Bay View Library to Botany Gardens?

    How far is it from Botany Gardens to the Chamber of Commerce?

    How far is it from the Chamber of Commerce to San Felipe Park?

    How far is it from San Felipe Park to the swimming pool?

    How far is it from the swimming pool to the train station?

Here are some other ways to say how far places are. Use them in your answers:

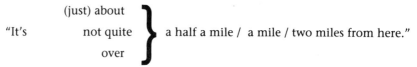

E   Here is a grid map of the United States and southern Canada.

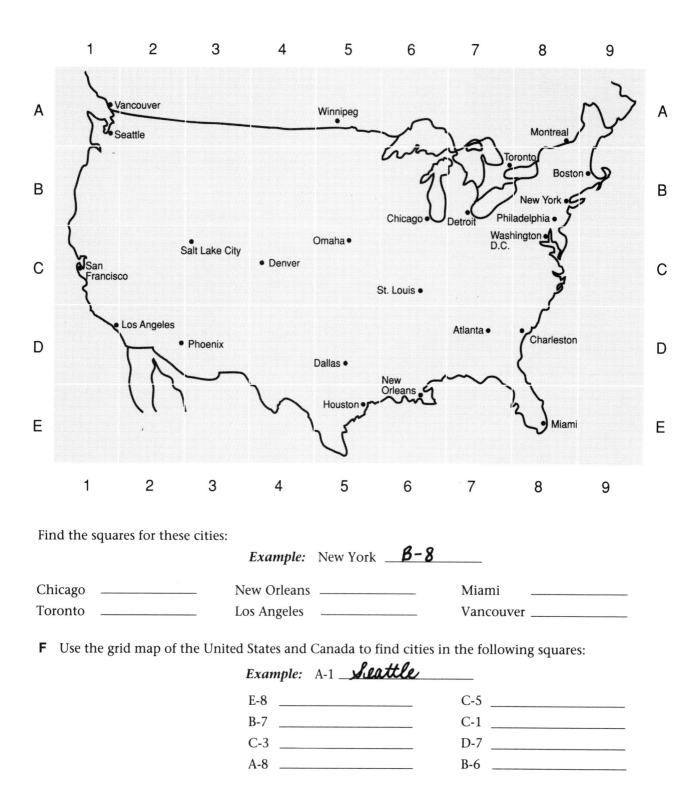

Find the squares for these cities:

Example: New York __*B-8*__

Chicago _____   New Orleans _____   Miami _____

Toronto _____   Los Angeles _____   Vancouver _____

F   Use the grid map of the United States and Canada to find cities in the following squares:

Example: A-1 __*Seattle*__

E-8 _____   C-5 _____

B-7 _____   C-1 _____

C-3 _____   D-7 _____

A-8 _____   B-6 _____

G   Look at the list of states and provinces below. First, match each state or province with its abbreviation. Then put them in alphabetical order, beginning with Alberta.

Texas	ME
Tennessee	AZ
Ontario	TX
Arizona	NY
Illinois	TN
Maine	IL
Washington	BC
Alberta	CA
New York	WA
California	ON
British Columbia	FL
Florida	AB

H   Read this address:

450 South Liberty Avenue
Apartment 305
Pittsburgh, Pennsylvania 15213

Here is the same address with some abbreviations. Can you find them?

450 S. Liberty Ave. Apt. 305
Pittsburgh, PA 15213

Rewrite this address using abbreviations:

670 York Avenue, Apartment 403
Toronto, Ontario M4N 3MC

Rewrite this address using complete words:

1681 N.W. Palm St., Apt. 201
Plantation, FL 32106

3 REVIEW

A Look quickly at the following **weather report** from a newspaper and find a map, an index, and a key.

The Weather

Index

Area 1: Seattle, San Francisco, Los Angeles, Tijuana
Area 2: Salt Lake City, Denver, Albuquerque
Area 3: Kansas City, Dallas, New Orleans
Area 4: Minneapolis, Omaha
Area 5: Detroit, Chicago, Toronto
Area 6: Washington, D.C., Atlanta
Area 7: Boston, New York, Pittsburgh

Area Forecasts

Area 1: Sunny; rain in some parts
Area 2: Partly cloudy; thunderstorms in some parts
Area 3: Sunny and warm
Area 4: Sunny and warm; windy in some parts
Area 5: Mostly sunny; brief showers in some parts
Area 6: Humid and cloudy
Area 7: Cloudy; thunderstorms in some parts

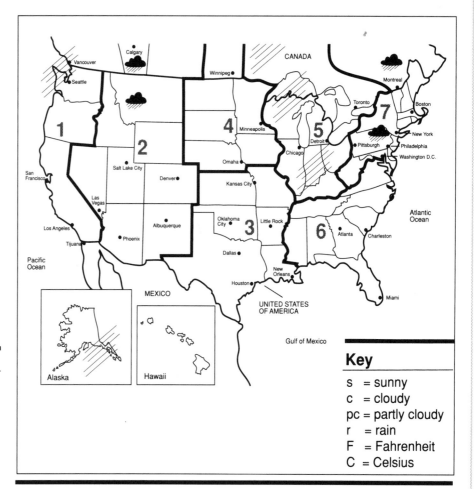

Key

s = sunny
c = cloudy
pc = partly cloudy
r = rain
F = Fahrenheit
C = Celsius

World Weather Chart

Cities	C	F			C	F	
Acapulco	32	90	s	Madrid	20	68	c
Athens	29	84	s	Mexico City	23	73	c
Berlin	17	62	r	Montreal	11	52	c
Buenos Aires	18	64	c	Moscow	21	70	c
Cairo	31	88	s	Paris	11	52	r
Calgary	24	76	pc	Beijing	29	84	s
Geneva	13	56	c	Rio de Janeiro	29	84	s
Hong Kong	31	88	c	Rome	20	68	pc
Lima	26	78	c	Sydney	23	73	c
London	15	59	s	Tokyo	27	80	r

B Now look at the weather report again. Then, with a friend, ask and answer the questions about the weather.

Examples:

North America   A: Where's Los Angeles?

B: (check map index) It's in Area 1.

A: What's the weather like?

B: (check Area Forecasts) It's sunny.

The world   A: What's the temperature in Acapulco?

B: (check World Weather Chart) It's 90 degrees Fahrenheit.

A: What's the weather like?

B: (check Key) It's sunny.

4 SKILLS CHECK

You have read   a street map
an index
a grid map
a scale of miles
a key
a weather report

You have practiced   using an index and a key to read maps
alphabetizing
reading abbreviations and charts

You have used these words and expressions

abbreviation
grid map
index
key
location
map
scale of miles
square
weather report
scan
schedule

3 DIRECTIONS

1 READING

Machiko is ready to leave the apartment and asks Sue for **directions**.

SUE: Hurry! You'll be late!

MACHIKO: But I don't know where to go!

SUE: Don't worry. It's not far.

MACHIKO: But how do I get there?

SUE: It's easy. Turn right on Grove. Go straight past Foothill and Green and you'll see an elementary school on your right. Then turn left at Prospect. The college is two blocks down on your left.

But Machiko got lost. A few minutes later she stopped, and thought . . .

MACHIKO: *(To herself)* Oh no, I'm lost. Did Sue say "go straight past" or "go left" on Foothill? I can't remember. *(She asks a man standing nearby.)* Excuse me. Can you help me? I'm looking for Bay View Community College.

MAN: It isn't far from here. Go back to Grove. Turn left and go about three blocks to Prospect. Turn left again. You'll see it on your . . .

MACHIKO: Just a minute please! Turn left on Grove, then go three blocks . . .

MAN: Yes. Then turn left again on Prospect.

MACHIKO: OK . . .

MAN: And the college is on the left.

MACHIKO: Thanks. I hope I get there this time!

2 PRACTICE

A This street map shows four places:

   A Sue's apartment

   B the elementary school

   C where Machiko got lost

   D Bay View Community College

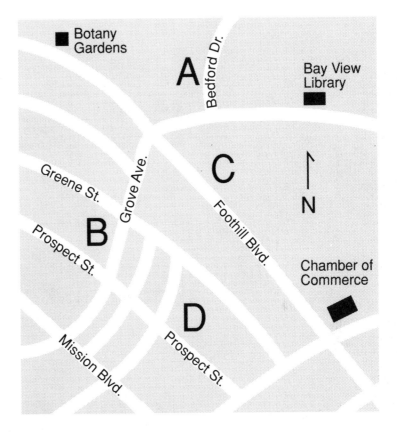

With a pencil, follow Sue's directions:

> "When you get out of the house, go to Grove and turn right. Go straight past Foothill and you'll see an elementary school on your right. Then turn left. The college is two blocks farther."

Now, with the pencil, follow Machiko's mistakes.

> She went to Grove and turned right. She went straight on Grove and took the first turn on the left. She walked about one block and stopped.

Where is the elementary school?

What mistake did Machiko make?

B   This **diagram** means "turn left."

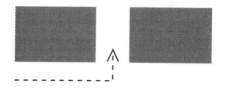

Can you match the following diagrams with their **written directions**?

"Take the second turn on your left."
"Go straight for three blocks."
"Turn right."

1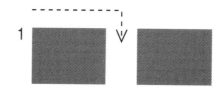

2

3

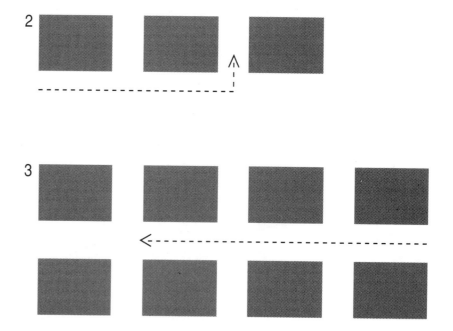

C   Draw a map from your home to the nearest school, bus stop, or park. Then write some directions in English to match your map.

D   Look at the map of Texas. El Paso is in the west part of Texas. Dallas is in the northeast part of Texas.

Where are: Houston?   Corpus Christi?
              Amarillo?   San Antonio?   Lubbock?

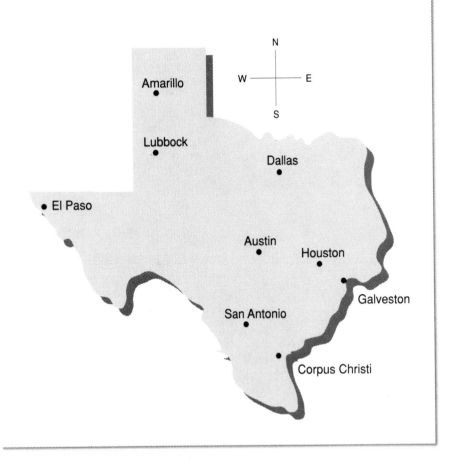

Houston is northeast of San Antonio. Where is:

Amarillo from Lubbock?   Austin from Dallas?
El Paso from Austin?   Corpus Christi from Houston?

E Use the following chart to tell a friend, as quickly as you can, where places are. Ask and answer questions like this:

A: Where's Minneapolis?
B: Minneapolis is 1218 miles northwest of New Orleans.

DESTINATION	DISTANCE	DIRECTION	START
Atlanta	688 miles	NW	Miami
Boston	219 miles	NE	New York City
Chicago	2113 miles	NE	Los Angeles
Denver	1059 miles	SW	Winnipeg
Minneapolis	1218 miles	NW	New Orleans
Montreal	582 miles	NE	Washington, D.C.
New York City	2996 miles	NE	San Francisco
San Francisco	754 miles	SW	Salt Lake City
Seattle	570 miles	SW	Calgary
Vancouver	1253 miles	NW	Albuquerque

3 REVIEW

Here is a **floor plan** of the de Young Museum and a message about two people meeting there.

> Dear Peter,
>
> Meet me in the cafe of the de Young Museum. Go to the main entrance. Walk straight ahead until you get to the Hearst Court entrance. Turn right, then take the next left. Go straight ahead, past the American Glass exhibit. Turn right into the British Art gallery and walk through it and the next two rooms. See you there at 11 a.m.!
>
> Sue

A   Follow the directions in the message by reading the floor plan.

B   Use the floor plan and the key to give written or spoken directions for these places:

   from the main entrance to the information desk.
   from the bookshop to the El Greco room.
   from the men's restroom to the Hearst Court.
   from the Nineteenth-Century Europe room to the Ancient World room.
   from the cafe to the telephone.

You can use phrases like:

Turn	left		Continue	into
	right			as far as
				until you see
Go straight	ahead			
	through			

Floor Plan

THE FINE ARTS MUSEUMS OF SAN FRANCISCO

M. H. de Young Memorial Museum

⭐ ARCHIVES OF AMERICAN ART

♨ CHECKING

📖 BOOKSHOP

📞 TELEPHONES

🚺 WOMEN

🚹 MEN

🍴 CAFE de YOUNG

❓ INFORMATION

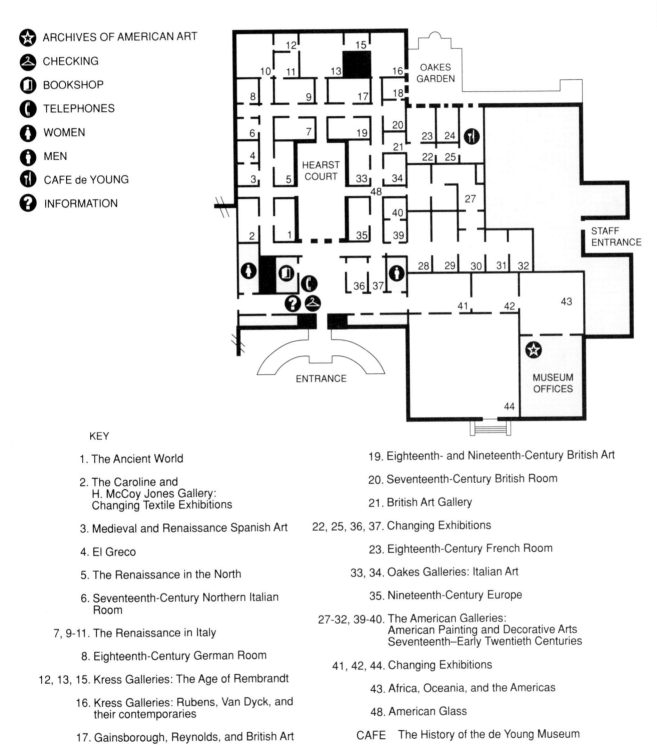

KEY

1. The Ancient World

2. The Caroline and
   H. McCoy Jones Gallery:
   Changing Textile Exhibitions

3. Medieval and Renaissance Spanish Art

4. El Greco

5. The Renaissance in the North

6. Seventeenth-Century Northern Italian
   Room

7, 9-11. The Renaissance in Italy

8. Eighteenth-Century German Room

12, 13, 15. Kress Galleries: The Age of Rembrandt

16. Kress Galleries: Rubens, Van Dyck, and
    their contemporaries

17. Gainsborough, Reynolds, and British Art

18. Eighteenth-Century English Room

19. Eighteenth- and Nineteenth-Century British Art

20. Seventeenth-Century British Room

21. British Art Gallery

22, 25, 36, 37. Changing Exhibitions

23. Eighteenth-Century French Room

33, 34. Oakes Galleries: Italian Art

35. Nineteenth-Century Europe

27-32, 39-40. The American Galleries:
    American Painting and Decorative Arts
    Seventeenth–Early Twentieth Centuries

41, 42, 44. Changing Exhibitions

43. Africa, Oceania, and the Americas

48. American Glass

CAFE   The History of the de Young Museum

4 SKILLS CHECK ✔

You have read   spoken directions
                       diagrams giving directions
                       written directions
                       a street map
                       a floor plan and key

You have practiced   reading directions
                       reading abbreviations for directions and distance
                       using floor plans and diagrams to give directions
                       following directions on a street map and on a
                       floor plan

You have used these words and expressions:

destination
diagram
directions
distance
floor plan
message

4 JOURNEYS

1 READING

Sue went to the museum to meet Peter. She used the BART (Bay Area Rapid Transit) system to get there. First, she went to the Hayward station and got a **subway map** of the BART system. Then she got on the Richmond/Fremont line and traveled northwest from Hayward. At the sixth station – Oakland City Center (a transfer station) – Sue got off the Richmond/Fremont line and got on the Concord/Daly City line. She traveled southwest and counted the stations again. At the fifth stop, which was Civic Center, she got off.

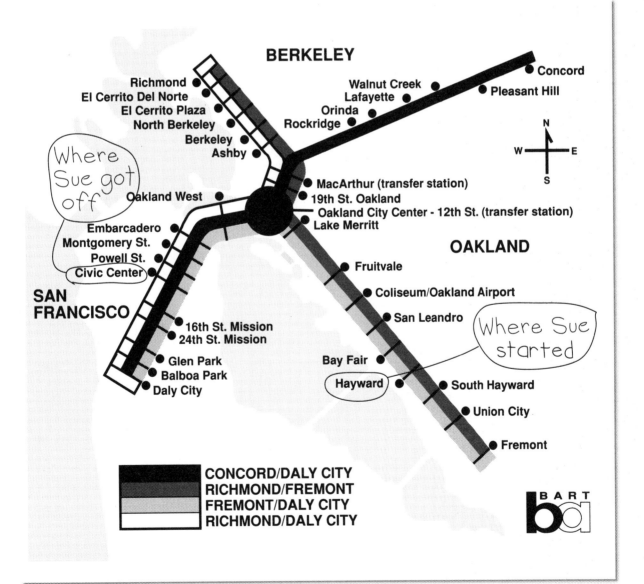

A   Follow Sue's trip from Hayward to Oakland City Center to Civic Center on the BART subway map.

B   In order to go from Hayward to Civic Center, Sue didn't have to transfer. Which line would have taken her there without her having to transfer?

2   PRACTICE

A   Sue counted the stations because she wanted to be sure to get off the train at the right stop. When the train stopped at the stations, Sue could see only part of the place names.

At which station was Sue when she saw:

ay Fa   
ale
ke Mer
adero
ell S

B   Sue traveled first on the Richmond/Fremont line. The 19th Street Oakland station is on the Richmond/Fremont line and also on the Concord /Daly City line.

Which line, or lines, are these stations on?

   Walnut Creek
   North Berkeley
   Balboa Park
   Lake Merritt

C   To go from Hayward to Civic Center, Sue got on the Richmond/ Fremont line and at Oakland City Center she transferred to the Concord/Daly City line.

Which lines would she get on and transfer to for these trips?

   Lafayette to Fruitvale
   El Cerrito Del Norte to Concord
   Richmond to Pleasant Hill

D   The San Francisco Bay Area is divided into east and west by the San Francisco Bay.

Are these stations east or west of the bay?

   Glen Park
   Powell Street
   Union City
   Coliseum/Oakland Airport

E Look at these directions:

In symbols:

In words:

From Montgomery Street station, take the Concord/Daly City line to the MacArthur transfer station. Transfer to the Richmond/Fremont line and get off at Berkeley.

Express these directions in words:

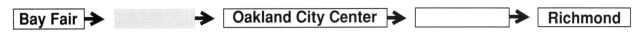

F Before Sue got on the subway, she picked up a **guide to parks** in the local area. Here is a page of the guide. Read the **symbols** and their meanings.

Beaches   Bicycling   Boating   Camping   Fishing   Hiking   Horseback trails

      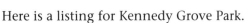

Jogging trails   Lakes/ponds   Picnicking   Softball   Swimming   Volleyball

Here is a listing for Kennedy Grove Park.

Kennedy Grove Park:

It means:

At Kennedy Grove Park there is picnicking. You can also go horseback riding and play volleyball.

Now read these symbols and describe the parks in the same way.

Redwood Park

Bay View Park

Sunset Park

3 REVIEW

A Machiko's sister attends Santa Rosa Junior College. She and Machiko visited San Francisco. Afterward, Machiko's sister returned by bus from the San Francisco Civic Center to Santa Rosa Junior College.

80 **Route 80, SANTA ROSA — Northbound**
San Francisco — San Rafael — Novato — Petaluma — Cotati — Rohnert Park — Santa Rosa
Monday through Friday except Holidays

80NoM F	Route	San Francisco Transbay Terminal	San Francisco Civic Center (7th & Market)	Arrive San Rafael (4th & Hetherton)	Leave San Rafael (4th & Hetherton)	Novato (Redwood & Grant)	Petaluma Depot (4th & C)	Cotati (Hub)	Rohnert Park (R.P. Expwy. & Commerce Blvd.)	Santa Rosa Transit Mall (2nd St. & Santa Rosa Ave.)	Santa Rosa Junior College	Golden Gate Transit (Piner & Industrial)
#•	80	5 23	5 30	6 10	6 10	6 29	6 48	7 04	7 10	7 22	7 27	7 34
•	80	6 01	6 08	6 48	6 52	7 11	7 30	7 46	7 52	8 04	8 09	8 16
•	70	6 31	6 38	7 18	7 22	7 41						
•	60	6 57	7 04	7 46								
•	80	6 59	7 06	7 48	7 52	8 11	8 30	8 46	8 52	9 04	9 09	9 16
	70	7 27	7 36	8 18	8 22	8 41						
	70		8 04	8 46	8 48	9 09						
•	80	7 57	8 06	8 48	8 52	9 13	9 32	9 48	9 54	10 06	10 11	10 18
	60	8 27	8 36	9 18								
•	80	8 57	9 06	9 48	9 52	10 13	10 32	10 48	10 54	11 06	11 11	11 18
	60	9 27	9 36	10 18								
•	80	9 57	10 06	10 48	10 52	11 13	11 32	11 48	11 54	12 06	12 11	12 18
	60	10 27	10 36	11 18								
•	80	10 57	11 06	11 48	11 52	12 13	12 32	12 48	12 54	1 06	1 11	1 18
	60	11 27	11 36	12 18	—	—	—	—	—	—	—	—
•	80	11 57	12 06	12 48	12 52	1 13	1 32	1 48	1 54	2 06	2 11	2 18
•	80	12 27	12 36	1 18	1 22	1 43	2 02	2 18	2 24	2 36	2 41	2 48
•	70	12 55	1 04	1 46	1 48	2 09	—	—	—	—	—	—
•	80	12 57	1 06	1 48	1 52	2 13	2 32	2 48	2 54	3 06	3 11	3 18
•	70	1 25	1 34	2 16	2 18	2 39	—	—	—	—	—	—
•	80	1 27	1 36	2 18	2 22	2 43	3 02	3 18	3 24	3 36	3 41	3 48
	60	1 53	2 02	2 44	—	—	—	—	—	—	—	—
•	80	1 57	2 06	2 48	2 52	3 13	3 32	3 48	3 54	4 06	4 11	4 18
	60	2 23	2 32	3 14	—	—	—	—	—	—	—	—
•	80	2 27	2 36	3 18	3 22	3 43	4 02	4 18	4 24	4 36	4 41	4 48
•	80	2 51	3 03	3 48	3 52	4 16	4 35	4 51	4 57	5 09	5 14	5 21
	60	3 17	3 29	4 14	—	—	—	—	—	—	—	—
•	80	3 21	3 33	4 18	4 22	4 48	5 07	5 23	5 29	5 41	5 46	5 53
	60	3 49	4 01	4 46	—	—	—	—	—	—	—	—
•	80	3 51	4 03	4 48	4 52	5 18	5 37	5 53	5 59	6 11	6 16	6 23
•	80	4 21	4 33	5 18	5 22	5 48	6 07	6 23	6 29	6 41	6 46	6 53
•	80	4 51	5 03	5 48	5 52	6 16	6 35	6 51	6 57	7 09	7 14	7 21
•	80	5 21	5 33	6 18	6 22	6 43	7 02	7 18	7 24	7 36	7 41	7 48
	70	5 55	6 04	6 46	6 48	7 09	—	—	—	—	—	—
•	80	5 57	6 06	6 48	6 52	7 13	7 32	7 48	7 54	8 06	8 11	8 18
•	80	6 27	6 36	7 18	7 22	7 42	8 01	8 17	8 23	8 34	8 39	8 44
	70	6 53	7 02	7 44	7 46	8 06						
•	80	6 57	7 06	7 48	7 52	8 12	8 31	8 47	8 53	9 04	9 09	9 14
•	80	7 27	7 36	8 18	8 22	8 42	9 01	9 17	9 23	9 34	9 39	9 44
•	80	7 57	8 06	8 48	8 52	9 12	9 31	9 47	9 53	10 04	10 09	10 14
•	80	8 59	9 06	9 48	9 52	10 12	10 31	10 47	10 53	11 04	11 09	11 14
•	80	9 59	10 06	10 48	10 52	11 11	11 29	11 44	11 49	12 00	12 04	12 09
•	80	10 59	11 06	11 48	11 52	12 11	12 29	12 44	12 49	1 00	1 04	1 09
★#•	80	12 33	12 40	1 20	1 20	1 42	1 59	2 14	2 19	2 30	2 34	2 39
★#•	80	2 03	2 10	2 50	2 50	3 12	3 29	3 44	3 49	4 00	4 04	4 09

Light type = am times   **Bold type = pm times**

Route 80 schedules serve all bus pads and the Golden Gate Bridge Toll Plaza.

★ These schedules also serve bus stops along Lincoln Avenue in San Rafael.

These schedules serve Marin City.

• ♿ The coaches on these schedules are equipped to accommodate wheelchairs.

80NoM F 871101 00 871016 01

Imagine you are at the San Francisco Civic Center. Ask and answer questions like these, using the **bus timetable**:

A: Is there a 12:36 bus to Santa Rosa Junior College every weekday?

B: Yes, there is.

A: Is there a bus at 9:00 a.m.?

B: No, but there's one at 9:06.

A: Is there wheelchair access to all buses to Santa Rosa Junior College?

B: Yes, there is.

B How quickly can you match these symbols with the words and expressions?

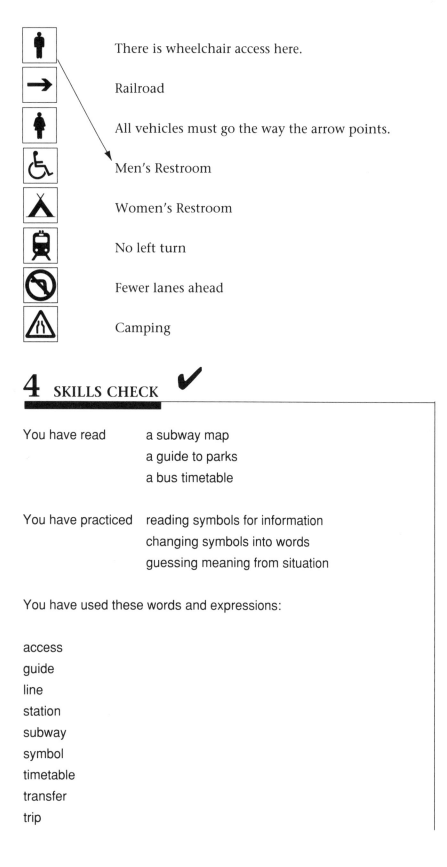

There is wheelchair access here.

Railroad

All vehicles must go the way the arrow points.

Men's Restroom

Women's Restroom

No left turn

Fewer lanes ahead

Camping

4 SKILLS CHECK ✔

You have read   a subway map
                     a guide to parks
                     a bus timetable

You have practiced   reading symbols for information
                     changing symbols into words
                     guessing meaning from situation

You have used these words and expressions:

access
guide
line
station
subway
symbol
timetable
transfer
trip

5 NOTICES

1 READING

When Machiko got to Bay View Community College, she found a lot of people there. She wondered what to do and where to go. At first, she stood with some other students in front of a bulletin board. On the bulletin board was a registration **directory**. She was going to ask the young man standing next to her for help, but he spoke to her first.

Bay View Community College Registration Directory

INFORMATION	Room 102
Hotel Management	103
Business Management	104
Science Courses (day)	106
Science Courses (night)	107
ALL NEW STUDENTS	110
Sociology	203
History	207
French	237
German	264
Spanish	276
OTHER FOREIGN LANGUAGES	281
English	290
Vocational Education	292
English as a Second Language (ESL)	310
Accounting	296
Drama	294
Art	311
Music	357
Physical Education	381
ALL OTHER COURSES	390

ROBERTO: Excuse me. Can you help me, please? I'm a new student and I want English classes.

MACHIKO: So do I.

ROBERTO: Oh! Are you a foreign student, too?

MACHIKO: Yes. I'm Japanese. You're Spanish, aren't you?

ROBERTO: No. I'm Brazilian, and I speak Portuguese.

MACHIKO: Well, I think we both go to Information in Room 102.

ROBERTO: But what about Room 110, New Students? We are both new first-year students.

MACHIKO: Yes, you're right . . . No, wait a minute. Let's look at the whole list first. . . .

ROBERTO: What about Room 290, English? Do you think that's right?

MACHIKO: No, look, farther down, near the bottom . . . English as a Second Language.

ROBERTO: That's it!

MACHIKO: OK. Let's go to Room 310. By the way, my name is Machiko Morita.

ROBERTO: I'm Roberto. Roberto Costa.

MACHIKO: Nice to meet you, Roberto.

ROBERTO: Nice to meet you too.

2 PRACTICE

A Check the **two** correct facts about Roberto and Machiko. They are

———— old students

———— new students

———— English students

———— foreign language students

———— English as a Second Language students

B Complete this sentence about Roberto and Machiko. Use these words:

English

Language

as

both

they

————— are ————— students of ————————— ————

a Second ————————— .

C Both Roberto and Machiko made a mistake. They both read slowly down the list of subjects and rooms in the registration directory instead of quickly reading the whole directory first.

What was the first word at which Machiko stopped reading?

What was the first word at which Roberto stopped reading?

D   Roberto and Machiko are students of English as a Second Language. They register in Room 310. Where do these students register?

Maria, a second-year accounting student

David, a student in his third year of Spanish studies

Ann, a student doing a second-year biology course in the evening

Carol, a second-year history student

Paul, a student from another college looking for his sister

Michael, a music student in his first year at the college

Laura, a bank manager interested in physical education

Yoko, a photography student

Barbara, a drama student in her second year

John, a new student of Russian

E   The room where ESL students register is on the third floor. Which floor are these rooms on?

business management

information

music

Chinese

daytime science courses

history

art

German

vocational education courses

hotel management

NOTICE TO ESL STUDENTS

Please sign up at the appropriate table.

COURSE	TABLE
Part-time course in English conversation	A
Full-time course in general English	B
Part-time course in general English	C
Part-time course in spoken English	D
Full-time course in written English	E
Full-time course in business English	F
Part-time course in business English	G

F   Roberto wants a *full-time* course in *business* English.

Machiko wants a *part-time* course in *general* English.

The relevant words for Robert are *full-time* and *business*.

The relevant words for Machiko are *part-time* and *general*.

In Room 310, they were given this **notice**.

Which table does Roberto want?

Which table does Machiko want?

G   Choose a word pair from the list on the next page. Then, as quickly as possible, *scan* the **job advertisements**. Do not try to read everything – just look for the words that are relevant to you. When you find the job that fits your two words, read the advertisement carefully.

Example: Your word pair is: film – language

Stop and read advertisement EO2.

Word Pairs

1. Part-time – Oakland
2. driver – overtime
3. college – technical

4. secretary – hospital
5. experienced – ESL
6. full-time – museum

Employment Opportunities

Medical secretary and receptionist urgently required for doctors in busy hospital. Perm. or temp. F/T or P/T. Call 930-0279.   EO1

ASSISTANT FILM EDITOR
needed, who speaks German or French, for the production of language courses. Full or part-time job. Call for appointment, 267-9619. EO2

PART-TIME evening work available in busy restaurant in Oakland. Friendly atmosphere. Ideal job for student. Call Richard after 6 p.m. at 921-8470.   EO3

Are you a good teacher? Position open for experienced teacher of ESL to teach evening classes. Send for application form to: Language Dept., Bay View Community College, 2995 Prospect St., Bay View, CA 94888.   EO4

HOUSE-CLEANING   work available   mornings/afternoons. Transportation provided, $30 per 4-hour session. 555-3453, days only.   EO5

Have you got TECHNICAL SKILLS? Do you like variety? Can you work under pressure? Small yet busy communications college urgently requires audio/visual aids technician. Apply in writing to Anderson College, Bay Rd., Alameda, CA.   EO6

Publicity assistant needed to work in State Folklore Museum. Full-time, good training and benefits, possibilities for growth. Salary commensurate with experience. Tel. 609-2128.   EO7

WANTED. Car park attendant. Must be excellent driver with experience with a wide range of vehicles. Work in shifts, 40 hours per week, overtime available. Full pay during training. Call for details and application form, 555-8246 (24-hour answering service).   EO8

H Here is a **list** of rules about examinations. Point 9 on the list will be important for a student who smokes. Which point (or points) are relevant to these people?

A student who is planning a vacation in June.

A student who does not have much money.

A student who likes to study at the college in the evening.

A student who is always late!

A student whose last bus leaves at 5 p.m. each day.

COLLEGE EXAMINATIONS INFORMATION

1. Examinations start June 16 and finish July 7.
2. Morning exams begin at 9:30 a.m.
3. Afternoon exams begin at 2 p.m.
4. All exams last 3 hours.
5. The college closes at 5:30 p.m. each day during exams.
6. Exam fees must be paid before June 1.
7. No student can enter the exam room more than 15 minutes after the beginning of an exam.
8. No dictionaries or other reference books may be used.
9. No smoking is allowed in exams.
10. No one may leave the room during the last 30 minutes of an exam.

3 REVIEW

A   Your friend is visiting a hospital. Use the hospital directory to get information about where to go.

HOSPITAL FLOOR DIRECTORY

First Floor		Second Floor
West	**East**	
Room 1 Admitting	Room 1 Gift Shop	Room 1 Community Relations
Room 2 Pharmacy	Room 2 Outpatient Clinic	Room 2 Nurses' Station
Room 3 Emergency	Room 3 Cashier	Room 3 Children's Ward
Room 4 Optometry	Room 4 Cafeteria	Room 4 Geriatric Ward
Room 5 Laboratory	Room 5 X-Ray	Room 5 Maternity Ward

Ask and answer questions like this:

Examples:

A: Where is the maternity ward?

B: Room 5, on the second floor.

A: Where do new patients go?

B: Room 1, first floor west.

A: Where do I go to get a prescription filled?

B: Room 2, first floor west.

B   Get information from this **schedule** of airport departures by reading quickly up and down columns and across rows, and by reading letters, numbers, and times.

AIRLINE	FLIGHT NUMBER	DESTINATION	DEPARTURE TIME
VARIG	861	Rio de Janeiro	10:00
AC	486	Montreal	10:10
AA	986	Mexico City	9:50
TWA	612	Seoul	10:25
PAN AM	786	Los Angeles	10:30
TWA	332	Madrid	10:35
AF	604	Paris	10:40
AM	622	Mexico City	10:50
QA	801	Sydney	10:55
JAL	205	Tokyo	11:00

How many TWA flights are there?
Where is Flight 604 going?
Which airline flies to Mexico City?
Which flight takes off at 10:55?
How many different destinations are there?
How many planes take off between 10:25 and 10:50?
Where is the Air Canada flight going?
When does Flight 986 take off?
How many different airlines are there?
When does the flight for Seoul take off?

4 SKILLS CHECK

You have read   directories
                     a notice
                     job advertisements
                     lists
                     a schedule

You have practiced scanning – reading quickly down and across looking
for relevant information.

You have used these words and expressions:

admissions
advertisement
bulletin board
columns
course
departure
directory
information
list
register
relevant
scan
schedule

Reading Review One

1 How quickly can you match these pairs? Match each item (A–Q) with its description (1–17).

> *Example:* A-5 is a correct pair – an alphabetical index.

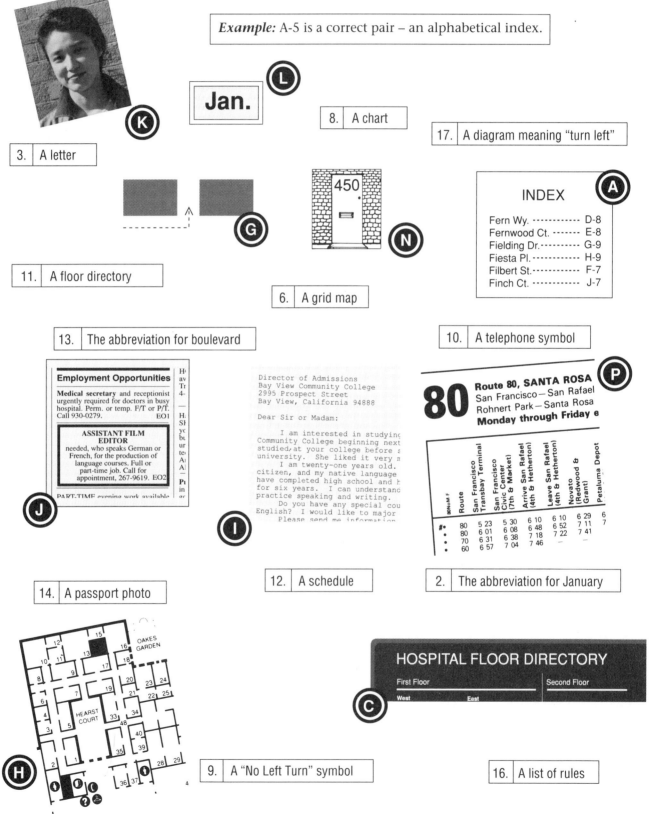

Ⓛ

Jan.

Ⓚ

| 3. | A letter |

| 8. | A chart |

| 17. | A diagram meaning "turn left" |

Ⓖ

Ⓝ

450

Ⓐ

INDEX

Fern Wy. ----------- D-8
Fernwood Ct. ------- E-8
Fielding Dr.--------- G-9
Fiesta Pl. ----------- H-9
Filbert St.----------- F-7
Finch Ct. ----------- J-7

| 11. | A floor directory |

| 6. | A grid map |

| 10. | A telephone symbol |

| 13. | The abbreviation for boulevard |

Employment Opportunities

Medical secretary and receptionist urgently required for doctors in busy hospital. Perm. or temp. F/T or P/T. Call 930-0279.   EO1

ASSISTANT FILM EDITOR
needed, who speaks German or French, for the production of language courses. Full or part-time job. Call for appointment, 267-9619. EO2

PART-TIME evening work available

Ⓙ

Director of Admissions
Bay View Community College
2995 Prospect Street
Bay View, California 94888

Dear Sir or Madam:

   I am interested in studying
Community College beginning next
studied at your college before s
university. She liked it very n
   I am twenty-one years old.
citizen, and my native language
have completed high school and h
for six years. I can understand
practice speaking and writing.
   Do you have any special cou
English? I would like to major
   Please send me information

Ⓘ

80 **Route 80, SANTA ROSA**
San Francisco — San Rafael
Rohnert Park — Santa Rosa
Monday through Friday e

Ⓟ

80Nо́M F	Route	San Francisco Transbay Terminal	San Francisco Civic Center (7th & Market)	Arrive San Rafael (4th & Hetherton)	Leave San Rafael (4th & Hetherton)	Novato (Redwood & Grant)	Petaluma Depot
#•	80	5 23	5 30	6 10	6 10	6 29	6
•	80	6 01	6 08	6 48	6 52	7 11	7
•	70	6 31	6 38	7 18	7 22	7 41	
•	60	6 57	7 04	7 46			

| 12. | A schedule |

| 2. | The abbreviation for January |

| 14. | A passport photo |

Ⓒ

HOSPITAL FLOOR DIRECTORY

First Floor   Second Floor

West   East

Ⓗ

| 9. | A "No Left Turn" symbol |

| 16. | A list of rules |

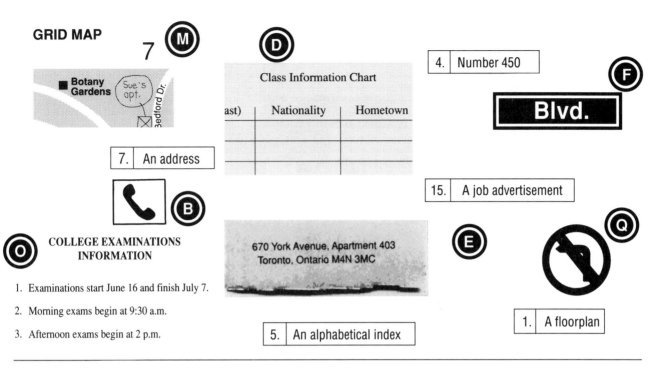

GRID MAP   7 Ⓜ

Ⓓ

4. Number 450

Ⓕ

Class Information Chart

7. An address

...ast)	Nationality	Hometown

Blvd.

📞 Ⓑ

15. A job advertisement

Ⓞ **COLLEGE EXAMINATIONS INFORMATION**

1. Examinations start June 16 and finish July 7.

2. Morning exams begin at 9:30 a.m.

3. Afternoon exams begin at 2 p.m.

670 York Avenue, Apartment 403
Toronto, Ontario M4N 3MC

Ⓔ   Ⓠ

1. A floorplan

5. An alphabetical index

---

2   How quickly can you solve these letter puzzles?

A   In this map are the names of some cities around the world. Two of them are the cities Roberto and Machiko come from. But the letters are in the wrong order. How quickly can you:

put the letters of each city in the correct order?
put the cities in alphabetical order?

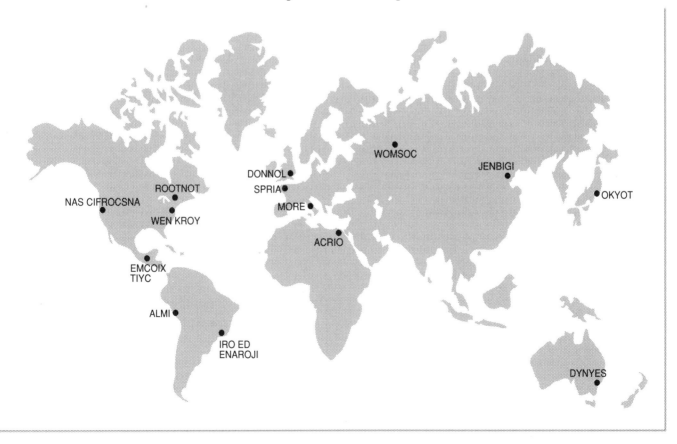

B   Complete this crossword puzzle.

Across

1 You can find Sue's *address* on her Employee Biography Form.

4 The abbreviation for "street" is _____ .

6 You can check your classmates' hobbies on the _____ on page 5.

7 There is a floor _____ of the de Young Art Museum on page 17.

8 The Student Record Card on page 4 is an example of a _____ .

9 Roberto wrote a letter to the college asking about the _____ for tuition.

10 What is the _____ for wheelchair access?

14 You can use the _____ on a grid map to locate a street.

16 Roberto would like to _____ in business.

18 The chart on page 15 shows the _____ between Seattle and Calgary.

19 The letter "W" is the abbreviation for _____ .

Down

2 On page 14, you looked at a *diagram* that meant "turn left."

3 To find out how far Prospect Street is from the Chamber of Commerce, you used a _____ of miles.

4 To _____ the job advertisements on page 27, you read quickly, looking for relevant words.

5 The abbreviation for the province of British Columbia is _____ .

7 You should use a _____ , not a pencil, to fill out important forms.

10 On page 8, you used a grid map to find what _____ each city is in.

11 Machiko and Roberto read the registration directory that was on the college bulletin _____ .

12 At Bay View Community College, there were _____ of rules and of subjects and rooms.

13 To read the abbreviations in the weather report, you had to use the _____ .

15 The abbreviation for "avenue" is _____ .

17 Sue got a subway _____ of the BART system.

PART TWO

Reading for Meaning

1 INSTRUCTIONS

1 READING

On the first day of school, Machiko and Roberto filled out **enrollment forms**. Here is Machiko's form.

English Department   BAY VIEW COMMUNITY COLLEGE
2335 Muir Hall

                                                      Enrollment Form C

PLEASE PRINT

1. Name (Ms.) _Morita_____ _Machiko_____
          Mr.
          Mrs.   Last   First   Middle
          Miss

2. Nationality   _Japanese_____
3. Native Language _Japanese_____
4. Local Address   _720 Bedford Ave._____
                    _Bay View, CA 94888_____
5. Phone Number   _(415) 555-8933_____

6. I have studied English   ☐ less than 1 year
    (check appropriate box)   ☐ 1—2 years
                                    ☑ 2—5 years
                                    ☐ more than 5 years

7. Term you are enrolling for: _F_ W Sp Sum
    (underline)
8. Do you have a part-time job?   YES   (NO)
    (circle YES or NO)
    If YES, how many hours per week? _____

9. How many hours of homework per week can you do?   ☐ 1 hour
    (check appropriate box)   ☐ 2—3 hours
                                                      ☑ 4—5 hours

10. Signature _Machiko Morita_____

FOR OFFICE USE ONLY - DO NOT WRITE IN THIS SECTION
Enrolled in _English 400____   Full-time   (Part-time)
Term (F) W Sp _Sum_   Fees paid #45.00 (By check) In cash
Student Ref. No. _55-0034987_____

2 PRACTICE

A   Here is an enrollment form for you to fill out. Be sure to follow the instructions correctly.

Example: CORRECT   (Check the appropriate box) ☑ 2–5 years
                        INCORRECT   (Circle YES or NO)   YES   ✓NO

Please Print

                    Ms.

1. Name (circle) Mr.   _____

                    Mrs.   Last   First   Middle

                    Miss

2. Nationality _____

3. Native Language _____

4. Local Address _____

                    _____

5. Phone Number _____

6. I have studied English
    (check appropriate box)
    ☐ less than 1 year
    ☐ 1—2 years
    ☐ 2—5 years
    ☐ more than 5 years

7. Do you have a part-time job?   YES   NO
    (circle YES or NO)
    If YES, how many hours per week?   _____

8. How many hours of homework per week can you do?   ☐ 1 hour
    (check appropriate box)   ☐ 2—3 hours
                                                       ☐ 4—5 hours

B Paul Murphy is going to Europe with his family. Read his **reservation form.**

C Answer these questions about Paul's form:

1. How many *children and infants* is Paul taking?
2. How many *rooms* does Paul want each night?
3. How long will Paul stay in *England*?

4. How much would accommodations cost *without* the children?
5. How much does Paul *still owe* Euro Tours? (Remember that he has paid a deposit.)

Euro Tours Inc.
Reservation Form

PLEASE PRINT

Name **Murphy**   **Paul**   **A.**
      Last   First   Middle Initial

Address **1823 24th Avenue, San Francisco, CA 94112**
Phone Number **527-8862**

Cities		Persons	No.	Rooms		
Which will you visit?						
City	**No. of nights**	Adults	**2**	**Type**	**No.**	**Bath** (CIRCLE)
Amsterdam				Single		YES NO
Athens	**2**	Children				
Florence	**3**	(3 - 14 yrs)	**2**	Twin		YES NO
London	**4**			(1 rm. 2 beds)		
Madrid		Infants				
Munich		(under 3 yrs)	**1**	Double		(YES) NO
Paris	**2**			(1 rm. 1 bed)	**1**	
Rome						
Venice				Triple		YES (NO)
Zurich				(1 rm. 3 beds)	**1**	

YOUR ACCOMMODATION COSTS			CHARGES (accommodation only)	
Per night:	Adult(s)	**$60**	Each adult	: $30 per night
	Child(ren)	**$40**	Each child	: $20 per night
	Bathroom(s)	**$10**	Each bathroom	: $10 per night
Total per night		**$110**	Infants	: FREE
Total no. of nights		**11**	N.B. Fares are separate	

TOTAL ACCOMMODATION COST	**$1210**	

I enclose a deposit of **$121**   SIGNED *Paul Murphy*

D   Now fill in the reservation form for Margaret Stocker and David Morris. (There is another blank form on page 123.)

Margaret Stocker

She lives at 1444 Riverside Drive, San Francisco, California. Her telephone number is (415) 882-3142. She will be traveling alone, and she wants a single room with a bath every night. She will be visiting London for six nights, Amsterdam for two nights, Munich for one night, and Paris for four nights.

David Morris

He lives at 282 East 44th Street, New York, New York. His phone number is (212) 998-6745. He will be traveling with his mother and his two children (ages 13 years and 2 years). They will be visiting Venice for three nights, Florence for four nights, and Rome for seven nights. Each night Mr. Morris wants two single rooms (both with bath), and one double room without bath.

Euro Tours Inc.
Reservation Form

PLEASE PRINT

Name _____

            Last   First   Middle Initial

Address _____

Phone Number _____

Cities		Persons	No.	Rooms		
Which will you visit?						
City	**No. of nights**	Adults		**Type**	**No.**	**Bath** (CIRCLE)
Amsterdam				Single		YES NO
Athens		Children				
Florence		(3 - 14 yrs)		Twin		YES NO
London				(1 rm. 2 beds)		
Madrid		Infants				
Munich		(under 3 yrs)		Double		YES NO
Paris				(1 rm. 1 bed)		
Rome						
Venice				Triple		YES NO
Zurich				(1 rm. 3 beds)		

YOUR ACCOMMODATION COSTS			CHARGES	
			(accommodation only)	
Per night:	Adult(s)		Each adult	: $30 per night
	Child(ren)		Each child	: $20 per night
	Bathroom(s)		Each bathroom	: $10 per night
Total per night			Infants	: FREE
Total no. of nights			N.B. Fares are separate	

TOTAL ACCOMMODATION COST	

I enclose a deposit of _____   SIGNED _____

3 REVIEW

A Here is a **questionnaire**. Make some copies of the blank question-naire, then fill out one copy yourself.

B Use the questionnaire to make a survey. Give the blank copies to classmates and to at least three people outside of class to fill out. Then answer these questions:

QUESTIONNAIRE ABOUT LEISURE TIME

Name _____

          (Please print)

Sex   (circle)   MALE   FEMALE

Which of these activities do you enjoy?
Check the appropriate column.

ACTIVITY	YES	NO
Participating in team sports		
Watching team sports		
Going to the theater		
Going to the movies		
Going to concerts		
Eating out		
Watching TV		
Listening to music		
Camping		
Bicycling		
Walking		
Jogging		

Please write down any other interests

_____

_____

_____

C Now put your answers on this **survey form**.

1. How many people filled out the questionnaire?
2. Which activity is the most popular?
3. Which activity is the least popular?
4. How many females answered?
5. Which activity is most popular with females?
6. Which activity is least popular with females?
7. How many males answered?
8. Which activity is most popular with males?
9. Which activity is least popular with males?

LEISURE TIME — RESULTS OF SURVEY

No. of forms		_____
No. of females		_____
No. of males		_____
MOST POPULAR	(all)	_____
	(F)	_____
	(M)	_____
LEAST POPULAR	(all)	_____
	(F)	_____
	(M)	_____

RESULTS (Write YES or NO)

Males and females
have the *same* interests   _____

Males and females
have *different* interests   _____

---

4 SKILLS CHECK ✔

You have read   an enrollment form
                     a reservation form
                     a questionnaire
                     a survey form

You have practiced   reading instructions on forms
                     reading abbreviations used on forms

You have used these words and expressions:

appropriate
check
circle
deposit
enrollment form
print
questionnaire
reservation form
survey
underline

2 MESSAGES

1 READING

At eleven o'clock in the morning, Machiko called Macy's Department Store, where Sue works. She wanted to speak to Sue. The switchboard operator answered the call.

OPERATOR: Good morning. Macy's. Can I help you?

MACHIKO: Yes, please. I'd like to speak to Sue Brown. She works in the shoe department.

OPERATOR: Please hold. I'll try that department . . . *(pause)* She's on break right now.

MACHIKO: Oh dear! Can you take a message?

OPERATOR: We don't usually do that . . .

MACHIKO: Oh, please! It's very important.

OPERATOR: Well, OK. I'm not too busy right now, so you can give me the message.

MACHIKO: Thanks. Tell her . . .

OPERATOR: Just a minute. What's her name again?

MACHIKO: Sue Brown. That's B-R-O-W-N.

OPERATOR: And what is your name?

MACHIKO: Machiko. M-A-C-H-I-K-O. I'm her roommate.

OPERATOR: OK. And what's the message?

MACHIKO: It's very important. Please tell her *not* to go back to the apartment after work.

OPERATOR: "Don't go back to the apartment." Yes?

MACHIKO: Tell her I've bought some theater tickets . . .

OPERATOR: "Theater tickets." OK.

MACHIKO: And tell her to be at the Bayside Theater . . .

OPERATOR: "The Bayside . . ."

MACHIKO: At seven o'clock tonight.

OPERATOR: "Seven o'clock." OK. I'll write this . . .

MACHIKO: Oh, wait just a minute. I almost forgot. Tell her to bring someone with her because I've got *four* tickets.

OPERATOR: "Bring someone." Is that all?

MACHIKO: Yes, thanks. She's in the shoe department.

OPERATOR: OK. I'll write out the message and send it to the shoe department.

MACHIKO: Thanks a lot. Goodbye.

OPERATOR: Goodbye. Enjoy the play.

2 PRACTICE

A Answer these questions about Machiko's message:

1. What does Machiko tell Sue *not* to do?

2. What does Machiko have?

3. Where should Sue go?

4. What time must Sue be there?

5. What else does Machiko tell Sue to do?

B Now look at these two different versions of Machiko's message.

These are the short, **informal notes** that the operator made while she was talking to Machiko.

Msg.   11 a.m.

Sue Brown

Fr. Rm. Mate Machiko

– v. imp.
– don't go back apt.
– M. has th. tkts.
– be at Bysd th. 7 p.m.
– br. S.O.
– 4 tkts.

Shoe

This is the complete **formal message** the operator wrote for Sue and sent to the shoe department.

To _Sue Brown – Shoe Dept._ ☐ URGENT
Date _Sept. 5_   Time _11 a.m._   A.M. P.M.

WHILE YOU WERE OUT

From _Machiko_

Of _____

Phone _____

Area Code			Number		Ext.
Telephoned	X		Please call		
Came to see you			Wants to see you		
Returned your call			Will call again		

Message _You received a phone call_
from your roommate Machiko. It's
very important. She said don't go
back to the apartment. She has
some theater tickets. She wants you
to be at the Bayside Theater at
7 o'clock this evening. Bring
someone – she has four tickets.

Signed _____

C Look at the operator's short notes. She has left out some words. She has also made some words shorter.

Examples: Msg. = message   fr. = from

Here are some more abbreviations:

rm.	s.o.	7 p.m.
apt.	v.	M.
tkts.	th.	br.
Bysd.	imp.	

For these abbreviations, find the complete words in the long message.

D   Sue's sister Beth owns a boutique (a small clothing store) and has a small son. Sometimes she has to go to Los Angeles on business. Her mother lives near her, and Beth likes to leave her son with her mother when she's away. One day, Beth stopped by her mother's house, but she wasn't home. Beth was in a hurry, so she wrote a note and pushed it under the door.

> *Dear M.*
>   *Came by early this aft.*
> *around 1. You weren't in !*
> *Thought you'd be in. Did you*
> *go shopping?*
>   *Wanted to ask you s.t.*
> *Can you pl. look after David*
> *this w.e.? Am going to L.A.*
> *on bus (Fri. a.m. – Sat. eve.)*
> *Will bring David Fri. 7:30 a.m.*
>   *Thanks! Talk to you soon.*
>   *Love,*
>   *B*
>
> *P.S. And D. wants to stay*
> *with his g.m. again!*

Read Beth's message and look for her abbreviations of these words:

something
weekend
business
please
Los Angeles

Beth has made her message shorter by:

1. Leaving out some words. For example, leaving out "I" from the beginning of sentences and leaving out some short words like "at" and "on."

Example: "will bring David Fri. 7:30 a.m." = "*I* will bring David *on* Friday *at* 7:30 a.m."

2. Using some common abbreviations.

Examples: a.m. = morning
              Fri. = Friday

3. Using some of her own abbreviations.

Examples: w.e. = weekend
              pl. = please

E   You know that Beth owns a boutique, has one son, and is going on a business trip. Use this information to guess the answers to these questions:

1. Who is "M"?

2. What does "aft." mean?

3. Where will Beth be on Friday?

4. What does "eve." mean?

5. How many days will Beth be away?

6. Who is "D."?

7. Who is "g.m."?

8. P.S. means "postscript." When is it used?

F   Write out Beth's message in full. Put in all the missing words, and write out the abbreviations in complete words.

Begin: *I came by early this afternoon around...*

G   Here is a note to Beth from Beth's mother. Put the missing words into the right places. Some of them are used more than once. The first missing word has been added.

on

the

to

at

I

*I*____ am happy to take David this weekend. Bring him _____ my

house _____ Friday morning. _____ will meet you _____ _____

airport_____ Saturday evening. Will you be _____ _____ 7 p.m.

flight?_____ will see you _____ Friday.

Love, M.

3 REVIEW

A This is an English **dictionary entry**. Can you find abbreviations for:

noun   something

somebody   slang

> **mess·age** /ˈmesɪdʒ/ *n* **1** piece of news, or a request, sent to sb: *Radio ~s told us that the ship was sinking. Will you take this ~ to my brother? Got the ~?* (sl) Have you understood? **2** sth announced by a prophet and said to be inspired social or moral; teaching: *the ~ of H G Wells to his age.* **mess·en·ger** /ˈmesɪndʒə(r)/ *n* person carrying a ~.

What is ~ a symbol for?

B This is a message in full. Can you make it shorter by using abbreviations for people, places, times, and dates?

```
Dear Roberto,
Your friend Bill telephoned at
nine-thirty this morning. He wanted
to tell you that he will be at the
Rialto Cinema this Friday night at
seven o'clock. He asked me to tell
you to be there early.
                        Michael
```

C This is a **telegram**. It is from Sue's brother Mark.

```
TELEGRAM SERVICE CENTER
MIDDLETOWN, VA. 22645            Western Union Telegram

4-567584939857S65484   57890 ICS EOPEUNKG VJFJK KFJWI
1 365849404894737238329 FKFDJKGJUEEG VMFJERUIERU DVMFEJUERW


IN  NEW  YORK.   PLANE  DELAYED.  FOG.   HOPE LEAVE  A.M.
TELL  MOM  NOT  TO  WORRY.

LOVE,


MARK

12:36 EST

MGMCOMP
```

Below is the same message in a telephone conversation. Can you put the information in the same order as it appears in the telegram? Begin: "I'm in New York."

"Tell Mom not to worry about me."
"because of the fog."
"I'm in New York."
"My plane is delayed"
"I hope to leave in the morning."

4 SKILLS CHECK

You have read   informal notes
                         a formal message
                         a dictionary entry
                         a telegram

You have practiced   reading notes by recognizing common
                              abbreviations
                         reading notes by guessing at other abbreviations
                         reading notes by putting in missing words
                         guessing meaning from context

You have used these words and expressions:

boutique
common abbreviations
delayed
dictionary entry
formal messages
informal notes
missing words
on a business trip
on business
postscript
switchboard operator
telegram

3 FACTS

1 READING

After enrolling, Machiko and Roberto looked at the student bulletin
board. It had a lot of **posters** and **notices** on it.

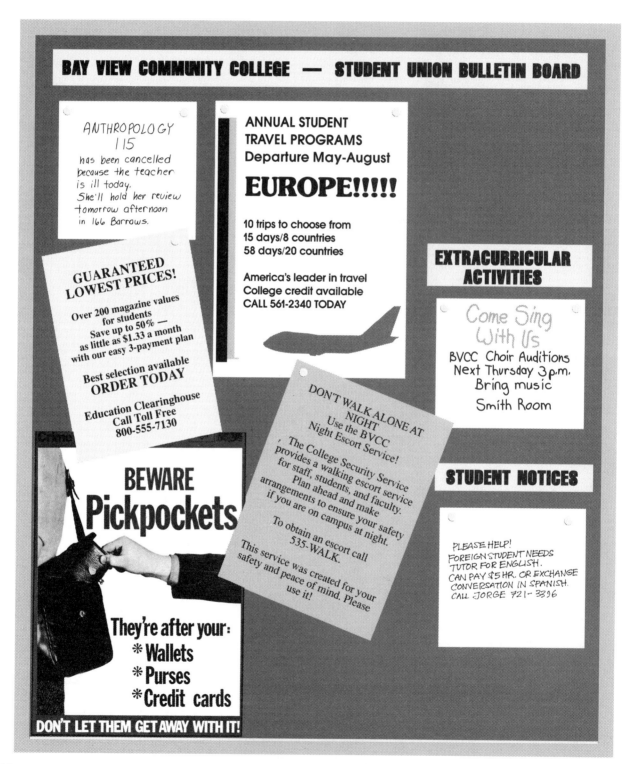

BAY VIEW COMMUNITY COLLEGE — STUDENT UNION BULLETIN BOARD

ANTHROPOLOGY
115
has been cancelled
because the teacher
is ill today.
She'll hold her review
tomorrow afternoon
in 166 Barrows.

ANNUAL STUDENT
TRAVEL PROGRAMS
Departure May-August

EUROPE!!!!!

10 trips to choose from
15 days/8 countries
58 days/20 countries

America's leader in travel
College credit available
CALL 561-2340 TODAY

**GUARANTEED
LOWEST PRICES!**

Over 200 magazine values
for students
Save up to 50% —
as little as $1.33 a month
with our easy 3-payment plan

Best selection available
ORDER TODAY

Education Clearinghouse
Call Toll Free
800-555-7130

EXTRACURRICULAR
ACTIVITIES

Come Sing
With Us
BVCC Choir Auditions
Next Thursday 3 p.m.
Bring music
Smith Room

DON'T WALK ALONE AT
NIGHT
Use the BVCC
Night Escort Service!
The College Security Service
provides a walking escort service
for staff, students, and faculty.
Plan ahead and make
arrangements to ensure your safety
if you are on campus at night.
To obtain an escort call
535-WALK.
This service was created for your
safety and peace of mind. Please
use it!

BEWARE
Pickpockets

STUDENT NOTICES

PLEASE HELP!
FOREIGN STUDENT NEEDS
TUTOR FOR ENGLISH.
CAN PAY $5 HR. OR EXCHANGE
CONVERSATION IN SPANISH.
CALL JORGE 721-3396

They're after your:
* Wallets
* Purses
* Credit cards

DON'T LET THEM GET AWAY WITH IT!

Machiko and Roberto look at the student bulletin board.

2 PRACTICE

A Look at (don't read!) the notices and posters quickly. They all use different kinds of writing:

large print—GUARANTEED LOWEST PRICES
small print—College credit available
handwriting— *choir auditions*

B Now read the notices and posters more carefully. They give information about:

time – Thursday 3 p.m.
place – 166 Barrows
cost – $5/hr.

1. When and where are the choir auditions being held?
2. How much can the foreign student pay for tutoring?
3. How much can you save on a magazine subscription?
4. When and where is the anthropology review session?

C Now think about the subject of each notice or poster. They have different purposes.
Find a notice or poster on the bulletin board that:

1. Tries to sell something – this is an advertisement
2. Gives information – this is an announcement
3. Asks for help – this is a request
4. Tells students to be careful – this is a warning

D Read the poster. Match the items listed below (the information and the purpose) to the poster.

INFORMATION
subject
date
time
place

PURPOSE

CONTINUING STUDENTS:

BE A BUDDY!!

Remember how hard it was adjusting to college? This spring, new students will need **your** help.

Please give your time to new freshmen and transfer students.
BE A BUDDY!

To sign up to be a buddy, just attend this meeting:
**December 4, 1—3 P.M.
Student Union Lounge**

E Read the poster about *Macbeth* and the special notice from Eileen
below. Then look at each of the following statements and say whether
they are true or false.

	TRUE	FALSE
1. *Macbeth* is by William Shakespeare.	T	
2. This production is by the California Shakespeare Company.		F
3. The box office number is 789-0043.		
4. The play will run for six nights.		
5. Each performance begins at 8 p.m.		
6. Students must pay for their tickets before February 5th.		
7. Three tickets cost $45.		
8. Eileen is a member of the BVCC English Club.		
9. Students should meet at the Student Union two hours before the performance.		

Following 9 sold-out performances in
Northern California

Shakespeare comes to San Francisco

Oregon
Shakespeare
Co.
Macbeth

*Exuberant,
colorful!*
Memorial Theater, downtown

FINAL WEEK:
Last 6 performances, Feb. 6 — 11 at 8 P.M.
Tickets $15
For further information, call the theater
789 - 0403

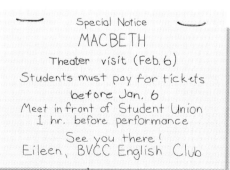

Special Notice
MACBETH
Theater visit (Feb. 6)
Students must pay for tickets
before Jan. 6
Meet in front of Student Union
1 hr. before performance
See you there!
Eileen, BVCC English Club

F   Read this poster and notice. Then answer the questions below.

What is the subject of the poster?

What is the purpose of the notice?

What are the dates of the circus?

What is the cost of the circus?

Where does Barbara think she left the tickets?

Find an example of: small print

large print

handwriting

G Here is a telephone conversation between you and Barbara Rabin. Read the entire conversation first. Then look back at Barbara's notice. You can then complete the missing parts of the telephone conversation.

BARBARA: Hello. This is Barbara Rabin.

YOU: _____

BARBARA: Oh, that's great! When did you find them?

YOU: _____

BARBARA: Yesterday morning? But I still had them yesterday morning. Where did you find them?

YOU: _____

BARBARA: In Lecture Hall II? But I lost them in Lecture Hall I! How many did you find?

YOU: _____

BARBARA: Four? For the 28th? Oh dear, they're not mine!

YOU: _____

BARBARA: I guess you could put a notice on the bulletin board like I did. Anyway, thanks for calling.

3 REVIEW

Make a notice or a poster, in English, to advertise an event in your school or neighborhood.

1. Use different kinds of writing: large print/small print/ handwriting.

2. Give clear information about: subject/dates/time/place/cost.

3. Include one of these: a request/a warning/an announcement/ an advertisement.

4 SKILLS CHECK

You have read	posters . . . that advertise
	. . . that warn
	notices . . . that request
	. . . that announce
	. . . that warn

You have practiced   reading for information
                                                  . . . about the date
                                                  . . . about the time
                                                  . . . about the place
                                                  . . . about the cost

                                           identifying the subject of posters
                                           recognizing kinds of writing
                                           answering true/false questions

You have used these words and expressions:

advertisement
announcement
bulletin board
cost
handwriting
large print
notice
place
poster
purpose
request
small print
subject
time
warning

4 OPINIONS

1 READING

Machiko and Roberto went to an art exhibit in the student center. Sometimes Machiko and Roberto agreed about the artwork, but sometimes they disagreed.

MACHIKO: I like this one. It's terrific.

ROBERTO: So do I. I love pictures of natural scenes.

ROBERTO: I don't like this one.

MACHIKO: Don't you? I think it's a very good abstract painting.

ROBERTO: Good? It's horrible, Machiko.

MACHIKO: Oh, I disagree. It's great.

MACHIKO: What about this portrait?

ROBERTO: I don't like portrait photography like that. I think it's terrible.

MACHIKO: I don't like it either. It's awful!

MACHIKO: This one is just silly!
ROBERTO: Silly? It's fantastic!
MACHIKO: I don't agree. I hate abstract sculpture. It's really bad.
ROBERTO: Oh, I like it a lot. I think it's the best artwork.
MACHIKO: Do you? I think it's the worst!

2 PRACTICE

A Do these quotations from the conversation express liking or disliking?

"I like this one."
"I hate . . ."
"I love pictures of . . ."
"I don't like . . ."

B Which three of these words express a "good" opinion?
terrific   awful   fantastic   great

Which of these words express a "bad" opinion?
terrible   silly   good   horrible

C Read the conversation again and find opposites for:
I hate   I like   bad   the best

D Look at the table. How many true statements can you make?

Machiko Roberto	likes dislikes	the natural scene
Both Machiko and Roberto	like	the portrait
Neither Machiko nor Roberto	likes	the abstract sculpture
Machiko and Roberto	agree about disagree about	the abstract painting

E Use some of the words from Machiko and Roberto's conversation to complete these conversations:

Agreeing

A: I like the picture
B: . . . . . do I.

A: I . . . . . the picture.
B: I don't either.

A: I . . . . . abstracts.
B: I agree.

Disagreeing

A: I like the picture. It's good.
B: Do you? I think it's . . . . .

A: I don't like the picture. It's awful.
B: . . . . . you? I think it's good.

A: I think the . . . . . is fantastic.
B: . . . . . ? It's terrible!

F Now have a conversation with a friend about one of the pictures in the reading. Follow this diagram:

Partner A   Partner B

Give an opinion ——→ Disagree

Disagree ←———— Give your opinion

G   Look at this **opinion page** from a magazine. Read the letter from the editor to the readers.

IN YOUR OPINION

TV VIOLENCE

"Violence on TV is definitely bad for children."

"The experts are wrong ... these programs are realistic and entertaining."

Dear Readers,
Last week I wrote about the subject of violence on TV. I gave you my opinion. I also wrote about the opinions of two professors — experts on the subject of TV and violence.

This past week many of you have written to me with your opinions. Here they are:

Dear Editor,
I agree with you. The experts are right! There is too much violence on TV. I hate programs about war, crime, and death, and I never watch them. They are terrible.

Violence on TV is definitely bad for children. My son and his friends watch violent programs, then they play very violent games. These games are horrible. I am sure that TV violence causes a lot of today's crimes.
— *Jim Anderson, Chico, California*

Dear Editor,
I don't agree with you about TV violence, and I think the "experts" are wrong. Violence on TV teaches kids about life. These programs are realistic and entertaining. This is good.

My husband and I love programs with action and suspense. We always watch them. They're great! Peaceful programs are dull.

I think a lot of today's crime is caused by bad parents, not TV.
— *Joyce Gordon, Winnipeg, Manitoba*

H Now read the letters to the editor on page 55.

Who *likes* programs with action and violence?

Who *dislikes* programs with violence?

Who *agrees* with the editor?

Who *disagrees* with her?

I Jim Anderson uses the word "terrible." Find another word in his letter that expresses the same opinion.

Joyce Gordon uses the word "good." Find another word in her letter that expresses the same opinion.

J In his letter, Jim Anderson uses the words:

death   hate   never   right   violent

Find five words in Joyce Gordon's letter with opposite meanings.

K Do you think the editor likes violence on TV? Give a reason.

Do you think the editor agrees with the experts? Give a reason.

3 REVIEW

A Read these two letters to the editors of a newsmagazine.

LETTERS

To the Editors:
I have been awed by the beautiful pictures taken from space of the moon, the earth, and the other planets, and I want to know more about the vast universe. We must invest our money to explore the unknown now. What will the human race do when earth's resources are used up? We could find ourselves trapped on a dying planet.
— Linda Miller, Tucson, Arizona

To the Editors:
Space cannot be the expensive playground of scientists and the military. If we stopped spending so much on space explorations we could reduce the national deficit or help feed the malnourished people of the world. Let's take care of our precious earth before we destroy other planets.
— Alan Adamson, Cape Canaveral, Florida

B   Which writer *likes* the current space exploration program?

Which writer *dislikes* the current space program?

C   Complete the two sentences about the writers by using these words:

beautiful   dying   expensive   malnourished

national   vast

1. Ms. Miller thinks the pictures of space are . . . and she wants to learn more about the . . . universe. She does not want to find herself on a . . . planet.

2. Mr. Anderson thinks space exploration is too . . . . He wants to spend his money to feed . . . people and reduce the . . . deficit.

4 SKILLS CHECK ✔

You have read	a conversation expressing opinions
	the opinion page of a magazine
	letters expressing agreement and disagreement
	letters expressing liking and disliking
You have practiced	reading opinions
	reading different reasons for opinions

You have used these words and expressions:

agree
awful
disagree
dislike
fantastic
horrible
like
opinion
opposite
peaceful
quotations
reasons
terrible
violence

5 PERSUASION

THE SALAD BOWL

Isn't it time to eat fresh fruit and vegetables at fair prices?

Enjoy delicious, nutritious, sun-ripened food and friendly, fast service at the most convenient restaurant in Bay View.

MENU
May we suggest…

1. FRESH FRUIT SALAD
Choose a small, regular, or large plate.
Fruit in season topped with cottage cheese, yogurt, or sherbet

2. PASTA AND VEGETABLE SALAD
Choose a regular or large plate.
Fresh spinach or egg pasta, with red ripe tomatoes, steamed broccoli, and green pepper, marinated in our own vinaigrette dressing

3. CHEF'S SALAD
Choose a regular or large plate.
Ham, chicken, beef, and four kinds of cheese (for the person with the hearty appetite!)

4. SOUP OF THE DAY
Choose a cup or bowl.
Made with the freshest ingredients and carefully seasoned

With your meal, enjoy a basket of fresh-baked bread and a glass of California wine. Choose from chilled white or rich ruby red.

Finish with a cup of freshly brewed coffee or a cup of tea.

Everything at THE SALAD BOWL is made the same day you eat it.

THE SALAD BOWL — famous for the freshest food at the fairest prices. Tell your friends about us and come again!

1 READING

At lunchtime, Machiko and Roberto were hungry. They found a restaurant near the college. The **menu** looked very good.

Machiko and Roberto chose a table at The Salad Bowl, sat down, and read the menu. Then they waited. They waited for a long time. At last a waiter came.

WAITER: Yes?
MACHIKO: I'd like a fruit salad, please.
WAITER: Cottage cheese, yogurt, or sherbet?
MACHIKO: Er – yogurt, please.
WAITER: Anything else?
MACHIKO: Yes. I'll have some bread and a glass of white wine.
WAITER: *(to Roberto)* And you?
ROBERTO: The chef's salad – large, with bread and white wine, please.
              (After the waiter left)
MACHIKO: The waiter was unfriendly, wasn't he?
ROBERTO: No, not unfriendly. He was rude!

Machiko and Roberto waited another ten minutes. Then their food arrived.

ROBERTO: Large? This is a small salad!
MACHIKO: And this is sherbet instead of yogurt.
ROBERTO: The bread is hard.
MACHIKO: It's not fresh at all, it's stale. I can't eat it.
ROBERTO: And I can't drink this wine. Chilled? It's warm!
MACHIKO: Terrible! There's no butter for the bread, either.
ROBERTO: Where's the waiter?
MACHIKO: I don't know. He's probably gone to lunch at another
              restaurant.

2 PRACTICE

A   Machiko and Roberto were persuaded to eat at The Salad Bowl by the language used in the menu. The menu uses a lot of words with "good" meanings.

Examples: *fresh* bread – not *stale* bread

                fast service – not *slow* service

Find five words here with "good" meanings and five words with "bad" meanings:

fresh	nutritious	friendly	terrible	famous
stale	hard	rude	delicious	unfriendly

Now use some of these words and others from the dialogue to say what was wrong with the lunch.

Example: Roberto's salad was not large, it was small.

What was wrong with:

     Roberto's wine? Machiko's salad? the bread? the service?

B   The menu also uses a lot of words about the same subject.

Example: *Small, regular, large* are all about size.

     Which three colors are mentioned?

     How many times is some form of the word "fresh" used?

Which one of these words is not about the subject of food and drink:

     tomato   salad   ripe   baked   fruit   season

Which one of these words is not about things that hold food and drink:

     glass   basket   plate   bowl   chilled   cup

C   The menu also uses a lot of words with the same sound.

Example: The sound /f/ is used five times in "**f**amous **f**or the **f**reshest **f**ood at the **f**airest prices."

     What sound is repeated in: "a basket of fresh bread"?

     What sound is used to describe: the tomatoes? the red wine?   the service?

D   The menu also uses:

questions   "Isn't it time . . . ?"

suggestions "May we suggest . . ."

instructions "Tell your friends . . ."

Are these questions, suggestions, instructions, or combinations of these?

1. May we suggest our chef's salad?
2. Do you want fresh pasta and vegetables?
3. Enjoy a glass of wine.
4. Choose from regular or large.
5. Finish with a cup of freshly brewed coffee.
6. Why not try our fresh fruit salad?
7. Come again!

E   Here is an **advertisement** from a magazine.

1. How many times can you find "cook" inside other words?

2. What type of pot do you need to use on the cooktop?

3. What two things make this cooktop better than others?

4. The picture shows a surface that is ready to boil water, but the person's hand is not getting burned. Can you explain why?

5. Here are four words from the advertisement:

   a. conventional   b. creating
   c. surface   d. efficient

   Match each word with a definition:

   outer part or top _____

   usual or traditional _____

   works well, without waste _____

   making or producing _____

6. Look at the last sentence. Does "get burned" mean "on fire" *or* "disappointed"?

The one thing Toshiba's new induction cooktop won't cook.

Believe it or not, this cooktop is ready to boil water. All it needs is an iron or steel pot. It works by creating a magnetic field that heats the inside of the pot—instead of the cooking surface. That makes it safer than conventional cooktops. And more energy efficient. So get yourself a Toshiba. Or you may get burned.

In Touch with Tomorrow
TOSHIBA
Toshiba America, Inc ,82 Totowa Road, Wayne, NJ 07470

F   Look at pages from a **travel brochure** and a **guidebook** about Hawaii.

from........a travel brochure ☞

There's no place on earth like the Hawaiian Islands.

You can explore the natural beauty of these tropical islands, enjoy a relaxing game of golf or a scenic boat ride, or visit Hawaii's historic museums.
Or you can simply sunbathe on the crystal white sand beaches.

This year, take your vacation in paradise —come to Hawaii!

from........a guide book ☞

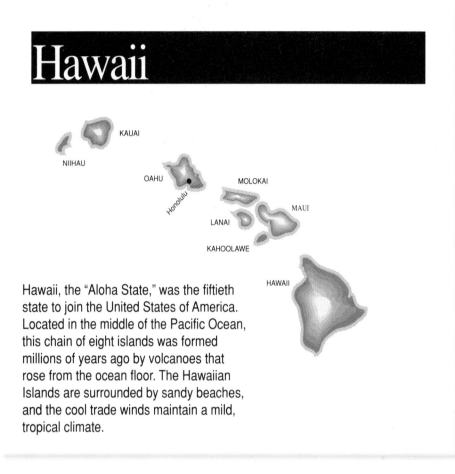

Hawaii

Hawaii, the "Aloha State," was the fiftieth state to join the United States of America. Located in the middle of the Pacific Ocean, this chain of eight islands was formed millions of years ago by volcanoes that rose from the ocean floor. The Hawaiian Islands are surrounded by sandy beaches, and the cool trade winds maintain a mild, tropical climate.

G   Now answer these questions about the pictures and words in each text on Hawaii.

1. Look at the illustration in each text.

   Which illustration gives information?

   Which illustration tries to persuade?

2. Look at the first sentence in each text.

   In which text does the first sentence give an opinion?

   In which text does the first sentence state a fact?

3. Now read both texts quickly.

   Which text tells how the Hawaiian Islands were made?

   Which text tells about things to do in Hawaii?

   Which words does each text use to describe the beaches?

3 REVIEW

A   Write an advertisement in English. You can use an illustration. In your advertisement, try to repeat words or sounds, choose words with "good" meanings, and use different words about the same subject.

B   Write a letter of complaint to The Salad Bowl restaurant from Roberto.

4 SKILLS CHECK ✔

You have read	a menu
	advertisements
	a travel brochure
	a guidebook
You have practiced	reading the language of persuasion
	recognizing word groups
	recognizing the use of repetition
	recognizing the use of illustrations

You have used these words and expressions:

complaint

fact

illustration

information

instructions

menu

opinion

persuade/persuasion

questions

repeat/repetition

same sound

suggestions

Reading Review Two

3 Monday	
4 Tuesday	*a.m. flight arrive San Francisco stay with D.*
5 Wednesday	*sightseeing*
6 Thursday	*shopping* *Bus station: L. Tahoe*
7 Friday	

1 Read this story twice.

A Read it quickly the first time.
B Read it again more carefully.

THE PACKAGE

Last week a friend stayed at my apartment. She arrived from Los Angeles on Tuesday morning, and she left San Francisco for Lake Tahoe on Thursday evening.

> M—
>
> See you at 5:30 p.m. at newsstand across from Union Sq. I'll go w/you to the bus station and help carry yr. luggage.
>
> Love,
> D

She wanted to do some shopping on Thursday morning. Before I went to work, I left her a message. I told her to meet me at half-past five, at   5
the newspaper stand across from Union Square. Then I would help her carry her luggage and shopping bag to the bus station.

I arrived at Union Square on time. I walked across the street to the newspaper stand. There were lots of people on the sidewalk. At first, I could not see Marie. I put my briefcase down. Then I heard Marie's   10
voice. "Hello, Dave!" she said. "Hi, Marie!" I answered. "We can walk to the bus station from here."

I picked up her suitcase and her shopping bag. In her shopping bag there was a big package wrapped in brown paper. It was very heavy. "Could you carry my briefcase, Marie?" I asked. "Of course," said Marie.   15
"Let's go!"

We walked down the street. It was very busy. The traffic was noisy. "The traffic's terrible," said Marie. "Yes, awful!" I shouted. "Thanks so much for helping me, Dave," said Marie. "Oh, that's all right, Marie," I answered. "You're carrying my briefcase." "But your package looks 20 very heavy!" said Marie.

I stopped. "*My* package?" I said. "It isn't my package. I thought it was yours. I thought it was what you bought shopping." "Oh no," said Marie. "I changed my mind. I didn't do any shopping. I didn't have time. It isn't my package, Dave," she said. "Then whose package is it?" 25 I asked. "I don't know!" answered Marie. We both laughed. "Let's open it and look," she suggested.

We opened the package. Inside, there were fifty copies of a Los Angeles magazine. I had picked them up at the newspaper stand! We both laughed again. 30

We took the package back to the newsstand. "I'm very sorry," I said to the man at the newspaper stand. "It was a mistake." He laughed too. "Look," he said, "it's a great magazine. Why don't you buy one?" I bought one of the magazines and gave it to Marie. "Thanks," said Marie, "but you can keep it. I read it last week in L.A.!" 35

2 Understanding Parts of the Story

A   Finding words and phrases.

First, scan quickly.

Who said:

"Let's go!"   "We can walk to the bus station from here."

"I changed my mind."   "Why don't you buy one?"

Then, stop and look closely.

Which lines do these quotations come from:

"Then whose package is it?"   "Yes, awful."

"Could you carry my briefcase, Marie?"   "It's a great magazine."

Where do these quotations come from:

"across from Union Sq."   "stay with D."

B   Recognizing language purpose.

"Why don't you buy one?" in line 33 is an example of a suggestion. Find an example of these:

an apology   a request   an abbreviation

an expression of agreement   an expression of opinion

3 Understanding the Whole Story

A Remembering details.

Answer these questions without looking at the story:

    Where did Dave and Marie arrange to meet?

    Why did they arrange to meet?

    What happened when they met?

    How did Dave learn about his mistake?

    What did they do with the package?

B Putting events in order.

Here are some notes on the events in the story, but they are in the wrong order. How quickly can you put them in the right order?

    They arranged to meet across from Union Square.

    They went back to the newsstand.

    They opened the package.

    Marie arrived in San Francisco to visit Dave.

    Dave waited near the newsstand.

    Dave picked up a suitcase and a shopping bag.

    Dave apologized.

    Marie said the package was not hers.

    She had already read it.

    They saw that the package was full of magazines.

    He gave his briefcase to Marie.

Now use your answers to write the story in 150 words, or tell it in about three minutes.

Reading for Pleasure

Reading for Pleasure

1 COMIC STRIPS AND CARTOONS

1 READING

After lunch, Machiko and Roberto stopped at a newsstand. They wanted something to read. First, they looked at some comic strips and cartoons in comic books, newspapers, and magazines. Here are some words about comic strips and cartoons:

a **cartoon**

a **comic strip**

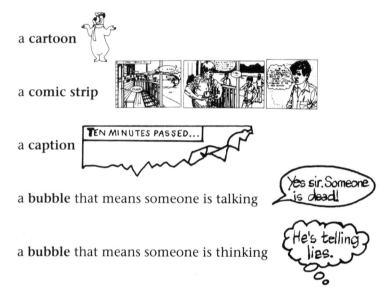

a **caption**

TEN MINUTES PASSED...

a **bubble** that means someone is talking

Yes sir. Someone is dead!

a **bubble** that means someone is thinking

He's telling lies.

Here is a comic strip about a man named Mallet. Mallet is investigating a robbery and a murder.

2 PRACTICE

A Choose the correct word in each of the following sentences. Each word is in the story.

Example: Some gold and silver coins/jewels are missing.

1. Kildale is one of the chief's friends/neighbors.
2. Kildale is a member of the police/government.
3. Briggs is Mallet's assistant/boss.
4. The dead person is a woman/man.
5. Delia Fish was a police sergeant/agent.

B Choose the correct word in each of the following sentences. The word is *not* in the story.

Example: Mallet is a criminal/policeman. (You know the correct answer because Mallet is investigating a murder and works with a police chief.)

1. The chief is happy/worried about the case.
2. Delia Fish was dark/fair.
3. Mallet says/thinks that Kildale is lying.
4. The report says Kildale is a thief/politician.
5. The report says Delia Fish's death was murder/suicide.
6. The police chief wants to stop/help Mallet on the Kildale case.

C Here is another comic strip. This one is about a mountain climbing accident. First read the captions and look at the pictures. Then match the words below with the bubbles to tell the story.

I'm going for help.
(Thinks) The rope . . .
Are you OK?
(Thinks) Will he get help in time?
No. I can't move. It's my leg.
Please hurry.
Help!

D Here is a simple comic strip without words. Look at the pictures and guess the words. You could use a warning, a question, and an apology.

3 REVIEW

Here are four cartoons. First, look at each cartoon and decide who the cartoon is for and what the cartoon is about. Put a check next to each correct answer. Then write a paragraph about each cartoon to explain your answers.

A This cartoon is from a comic book.

It is for: It is about:

1. adults   1. crime

2. teenagers   2. war

3. children   3. romance

B This cartoon is from a newspaper.

It is for: It is about:

1. employees   1. cars

2. students   2. politics

3. anyone   3. vacations

C   This cartoon is an illustration from a storybook.

It is for: It is from a story about:

1. little children   1. creatures from outer space

2. teenagers   2. animals who can talk

3. adults   3. a chocolate factory

D   This cartoon is from a comic book called "Star Battles."

It is for: It is about:

1. parents   1. cooking

2. children   2. skiing

3. anyone   3. science fiction

4   SKILLS CHECK ✔

You have read   comic strips

                              cartoons

You have practiced   reading pictures with words

                              using pictures to guess words

                              matching words with pictures to make a story

You have used these words and expressions:

apology

bubble

caption

cartoon

comic strip

2 MAGAZINES

1 READING

Roberto and Machiko decided to buy a magazine. They both like rock music, and they both like reading about people's lives. So they bought a magazine called *Rock On!* and started to read the **biographies** of a rock group called MetaFlash.

ROCK ON!

VOLUME NO.4: JULY 1990
MAGAZINE

NAME:
Mike Donovan

DATE OF BIRTH:
Dec. 10, 1962

PLACE OF BIRTH:
New York City

FIRST GROUP:
Donovan & Smith

INSTRUMENTS PLAYED:
Keyboards and guitar

WHERE DID YOU MEET THE
REST OF THE GROUP:
I met Liz while performing with
Richard Smith in 1985.

INFLUENCES:
Bob Dylan, blues, jazz

FAVORITE
GROUP(S)/ARTIST(S):
Steely Dan and The Band

FAVORITE ALBUM:
Miles Davis

WHERE DO YOU LIVE NOW:
New York City

ROCK ON!

STARFILE NO.4:
MetaFlash

NAME:
Liz Evans

DATE OF BIRTH:
Sept. 9, 1963

PLACE OF BIRTH:
New Haven, CT

FIRST GROUP:
MetaFlash

INSTRUMENTS PLAYED:
Guitar and keyboards

WHERE DID YOU MEET THE
REST OF THE GROUP:
At Bard College when I was 22

INFLUENCES:
Rolling Stones, Motown

FAVORITE
GROUP(S)/ARTIST(S):
Tina Turner, Michael Jackson,
and the Rolling Stones

FAVORITE ALBUM:
Jackson

WHERE DO YOU LIVE NOW:
New York City

NAME:
Mark Brinkley

DATE OF BIRTH:
April 21, 1964

PLACE OF BIRTH:
Philadelphia, PA

FIRST GROUP:
MetaFlash

INSTRUMENTS PLAYED:
Lead guitar

WHERE DID YOU MEET THE
REST OF THE GROUP:
Robert and I grew up
together; he introduced me to
Mike in 1987

FAVORITE
GROUP(S)/ARTIST(S):
U2

FAVORITE ALBUM:
Don't know

WHERE DO YOU LIVE NOW:
New York City

NAME:
Rita Brown

DATE OF BIRTH:
Feb. 11, 1964

PLACE OF BIRTH:
New Haven, CT

FIRST GROUP:
MetaFlash

INSTRUMENTS PLAYED:
Bass guitar

WHERE DID YOU MEET THE
REST OF THE GROUP:
While studying at Bard
College

FAVORITE
GROUP(S)/ARTIST(S):
David Bowie, Eurythmics,
Janis Joplin

FAVORITE ALBUM:
Anything by David Bowie

WHERE DO YOU LIVE NOW:
New York City

NAME:
Robert Wiseman

DATE OF BIRTH:
Feb. 20, 1964

PLACE OF BIRTH:
Philadelphia, PA

FIRST GROUP:
MetaFlash

INSTRUMENTS PLAYED:
Drums

WHERE DID YOU MEET THE REST OF THE
GROUP:
At Bard College

INFLUENCES:
Prince, Rolling Stones

FAVORITE GROUP(S)/ARTIST(S):
Prince

FAVORITE ALBUM:
Prince

WHERE DO YOU LIVE NOW:
New York City

ROCK ON!

STARFILE NO.4:
MetaFlash

NAME:
Mike Donovan

DATE OF BIRTH:
Dec. 10, 1962

PLACE OF BIRTH:
New York City

FIRST GROUP:
Donovan & Smith

INSTRUMENTS PLAYED:
Keyboards and guitar

WHERE DID YOU MEET THE
REST OF THE GROUP:
I met Liz while performing with
Richard Smith in 1985.

INFLUENCES:
Bob Dylan, blues, jazz

FAVORITE
GROUP(S)/ARTIST(S):
Steely Dan and The Band

FAVORITE ALBUM:
Kind of Blue, Miles Davis

WHERE DO YOU LIVE NOW:
New York City

NAME:
Liz Evans

DATE OF BIRTH:
Sept. 9, 1963

PLACE OF BIRTH:
New Haven, CT

FIRST GROUP:
MetaFlash

INSTRUMENTS PLAYED:
Guitar and keyboards

WHERE DID YOU MEET THE
REST OF THE GROUP:
At Bard College when I was 22

INFLUENCES:
Rolling Stones, Motown

FAVORITE
GROUPS(S)/ARTIST(S):
Tina Turner, Michael Jackson,
and the Rolling Stones

FAVORITE ALBUM:
Off the Wall, Michael Jackson

WHERE DO YOU LIVE NOW:
New York City

NAME:
Mark Brinkley

DATE OF BIRTH:
April 21, 1964

PLACE OF BIRTH:
Philadelphia, PA

FIRST GROUP:
MetaFlash

INSTRUMENTS PLAYED:
Lead guitar

WHERE DID YOU MEET THE
REST OF THE GROUP:
Robert and I grew up
together; he introduced me to
Mike in 1987

FAVORITE
GROUP(S)/ARTIST(S):
U2

FAVORITE ALBUM:
Don't know

WHERE DO YOU LIVE NOW:
New York City

NAME:
Rita Brown

DATE OF BIRTH:
Feb. 11, 1964

PLACE OF BIRTH:
New Haven, CT

FIRST GROUP:
MetaFlash

INSTRUMENTS PLAYED:
Bass guitar

WHERE DID YOU MEET THE
REST OF THE GROUP:
While studying at Bard
College

FAVORITE
GROUP(S)/ARTIST(S):
David Bowie, Eurythmics,
Janis Joplin

FAVORITE ALBUM:
Anything by David Bowie

WHERE DO YOU LIVE NOW:
New York City

NAME:
Robert Wiseman

DATE OF BIRTH:
Feb. 20, 1964

PLACE OF BIRTH:
Philadelphia, PA

FIRST GROUP:
MetaFlash

INSTRUMENTS PLAYED:
Drums

WHERE DID YOU MEET THE REST OF THE
GROUP:
At Bard College

INFLUENCES:
Prince, Rolling Stones

FAVORITE GROUP(S)/ARTIST(S):
Prince

FAVORITE ALBUM:
Purple Rain, Prince

WHERE DO YOU LIVE NOW:
New York City

2 PRACTICE

A Look at the first biography. It's about Mike Donovan. It tells you about:

Events in his life: He was born on December 10, 1962.
Facts about his life: He plays the keyboards and guitar.
People in his life: He used to perform with Richard Smith.
Opinions he has about music: His favorite groups are Steely Dan and The Band.

B Events. Answer these questions with a date.

Example: When was Mike Donovan born?
December 10, 1962

When was Rita Brown born?
When was Robert Wiseman born?
When did Liz Evans meet the rest of the group?
When did Mark Brinkley meet the rest of the group?
When did Mike Donovan meet Liz Evans?

C Facts. Say whether these sentences are true or false.

Mike Donovan was born in New Haven.
Rita Brown plays the bass guitar.
Liz Evans plays the drums.
Mark Brinkley was born in Long Island.
Mike Donovan is older than Mark Brinkley.
Rita Brown is older than Robert Wiseman.
The oldest member of MetaFlash is Mike Donovan.
All the members of MetaFlash now live in New York City.
David Bowie is the favorite artist of two members of MetaFlash.
Three members of MetaFlash attended Bard College.

D Now put some of the missing facts into this paragraph. The answers are all numbers.

MetaFlash is a group with _____ members. Only _____ member of the group was born in New York City, but he and the other _____ members all live there now. _____ of the members were born in the same town, and _____ members of the group went to the same college. Mike Donovan and Liz Evans play _____ instruments, but the others play only _____ .

E People and opinions. Put the missing words into these sentences. The answers are all names and titles.

Mike Donovan's favorite album is _____ .
Robert Wiseman's favorite album is _____ .
Rita Brown's favorite artists are _____ .
Liz Evan's favorite album is _____ .
_____ doesn't know what his favorite album is.

F Read this **magazine article** about Elvis Presley carefully.

THE KING IS DEAD:
LONG LIVE THE KING

Elvis Presley was born on January 8, 1935, in Tupelo, Mississippi. His parents were poor, and they were very religious. They often took Elvis to church. That's where he first learned to sing. Most people feel that these religious songs had a big influence on Elvis's singing style.

Then, when he was a teenager, Elvis went to live in Memphis, Tennessee. He went to the local high school. He was an average student. The thing he was really interested in was music

One day, in 1955, he took his guitar to the Sun Recording Studio in Memphis. There he recorded two country 'n' western songs for his mother's birthday. All her life she was very close to Elvis. One of the songs was called *That's All Right, Mama.* The recording studio liked the songs and they liked the singer. His style was a mixture of two traditions, white country 'n' western, and blues — the music of black people in the South.

A few months later, Elvis met "Colonel" Tom Parker. Parker took over Elvis's career. With his management, Elvis became popular not only in America but all over the world. Soon, Elvis had his first smash hits — *Hound Dog, All Shook Up*, and many others. They were wonderful songs, sung by the greatest pop star in the history of pop music.

Some years later, Elvis was making Hollywood films like *Love Me Tender* and *King Creole*. He made many films — some people say too many. Some of them were not very good. But Elvis's fans were always loyal. They went to see all his films and they bought all his records.

Elvis died at the age of 42. It was a sudden death and it came as a shock. Everyone knew Elvis was the king of rock 'n' roll. And everyone knows he will always be the king of rock 'n' roll. Long live Elvis!

G   Here are eight events in Elvis Presley's life, but they are in the wrong order. Can you put them in the right order?

Elvis recorded "That's All   He learned to sing in church.
   Right, Mama."   Elvis met "Colonel" Tom Parker.
Elvis died.   Elvis went to school in
He made his first hit records.   Memphis.
Elvis was born.   He made movies in Hollywood.

H   Now write a paragraph about the events in Elvis Presley's life. To do this, match each of the events from Exercise G with one of the following words and phrases about time. This will help you tell when each event happened. (You will also find words and phrases about time in the article about Elvis. Use them to help you.)

In your paragraph, put these words at the *beginning* of events:

   one day   soon   a few months later

   then   at first   some years later

Put these words at the *end* of events:

   suddenly   in 1935

I   Here are some facts and opinions about Elvis. Can you find four facts and three opinions?

   Elvis first recorded at Sun Recording Studio.
   They were wonderful songs.
   Elvis's manager was "Colonel" Tom Parker.
   Elvis made many films.
   Elvis made too many films.
   Elvis went to live in Memphis.
   Elvis will always be the king of rock 'n' roll.

J   Look at the first sentences in the article about Elvis Presley.

Elvis Presley was born on January 8, 1935, in Tupelo, Mississippi.

His parents were poor, and they were very religious.

"His" refers to Elvis Presley. "They" refers to his parents.

Here are some other people and events in Elvis's life:

   They often took Elvis to church.   Who were "they"?
   She was very close to Elvis.   Who was "she"?
   He took over Elvis's career.   Who was "he"?
   They went to see all his films.   Who were "they"?
   Some of them were not very good.   What are "them"?
   It came as a shock.   What was "it"?

3 REVIEW

Here is a paragraph about Elvis. But it does not make sense because the sentences are all in the wrong order. Use your understanding of the facts, events, people, and opinions in the article about Elvis to put the sentences in the right order. The outline that follows the paragraph will help you organize the sentences.

He helped Elvis's career enormously.   First, he had talent. What were the reasons for his success?   They will always remember him as King.   Second, he had a good manager.   Elvis Presley was born in the 1930s.   And third, Elvis has the most loyal fans in the world. Twenty years later, he was the world's most successful pop singer.   It was a talent for combining the music of white people with the music of black people.   Well, I can think of at least three.

Outline

1. Birth: _____

2. Success: _____

3. Reasons for success:

    a. _____

        Example: _____

    b. _____

        Example: _____

    c. _____

        Example: _____

4 SKILLS CHECK

You have read	biographies
	a magazine article

You have practiced	reading about events
	reading about facts
	recognizing words about people
	recognizing opinions

You have used these words and expressions:

article	opinions
biography	outline
events	perform
facts	shock
influence	success
manager	talent

3 NONFICTION

1 READING

After they left the newsstand, Roberto and Machiko bought a **guide book** called *This Is New York*. They both found it interesting. Roberto is going to New York soon to visit his friend Jack, and Machiko wants to go someday for a vacation.

Here are the parts of the book that they looked at and read.

1. The **cover** of the book
   The **title**
   The **author**

2. The **contents** of the book

CONTENTS

	pages
1. History of New York	2-7
2. Getting to Know New York	8-16
3. Things to See and Do	17-27
4. Infomation and Advice	28

3. The **introduction** to the book

INTRODUCTION

New York is the biggest city in ___1___ . More than eight
million people live and work in New York. Another four
million people live very near. Many of these people work
in New York, too.

New York is one of the most important cities in the
___2___ . It is a center for business. It is also a center for
music and ___3___ .

New York is an exciting city. It has many ___4___
buildings and places of interest. But New York is exciting
because of its people. They come from many different
___5___ of the world. Let us look at this unusual ___6___ .

---

4. Some **excerpts** from the book

Neighborhoods
To the north of Wall Street is *Chinatown*. Mott Street is the main
street of Chinatown. It is full of Chinese restaurants, vegetable
markets, and little shops. Many signs are in Chinese.

The Skyscrapers
From 1931 to 1970, the highest building in the world was the
Empire State Building. It is 102 stories high and there is a very
good view of the city from the top.

Shopping
Almost every avenue in Manhattan has stores. Most of the stores
on Madison Avenue are small boutiques. Many shops on Third
Avenue sell antiques.

New York's Parks
Central Park in Manhattan is used by thousands of New Yorkers
and visitors every day. Many of them like to walk in the Park.
Others like to ice-skate or go to the Zoo.

Museums
The most famous art museum in New York is the *Metropolitan
Museum of Art*. The Museum is in Central Park on Fifth Avenue.
It has great collections from all over the world. It also has a
concert hall.

Restaurants
Most restaurants in Chinatown are Chinese. There are many
Italian restaurants in Little Italy and many German restaurants
around East 86th Street.

2 PRACTICE

A   Look at the introduction again. Read the whole text and then guess the missing words. Here is an example and some clues to help you.

Example: Clue 1: The name of a country in North America

Answer: *The United States of America*

Clue 2: Another word for the earth

Answer:

Clue 3: People go to museums and galleries to see this

Answer:

Clue 4: Another word for "well-known"

Answer:

Clue 5: What Mexico, Japan, and Italy are

Answer:

Clue 6: Bigger than a town

Answer:

B   Look at the excerpts again. Guess which chapter you will find them in. You will need to look at the contents (p. 81) of the book.

Example: In which chapter will you find, "The first people in New York were American Indians"?

Answer: *Chapter 1, History of New York*

In which chapter will you find these?

1. "In 1626, one of the Dutch leaders bought Manhattan from the Indians. He gave them twenty-four dollars."

2. "It is easy to find your way in Manhattan. Most streets go east and west, and the avenues run north and south."

3. "Little Italy is north of Chinatown between Lafayette Street and the Bowery."

4. "There are also boat trips around Manhattan Island. Each trip takes about three hours."

5. "New York's most important zoo is in the Bronx. The Bronx Zoo is the largest zoo in America."

6. "Perhaps you will visit New York one day. Here is some advice."

C This is what Roberto and Machiko said as they were reading the book. Some of the words in the dialogue are missing. Use the excerpts from the guide book to help you guess the missing words. Six words are in the excerpts, and five are not. The first two words are done for you.

Example:

ROBERTO:	My friend Jack works on Wall Street.
MACHIKO:	I wonder if he ever goes to *Chinatown* . (from "Neighborhoods")
	It's not *far* from Wall Street. (a guess)

ROBERTO:	I don't think he has much free _____ .
MACHIKO:	Does he work in a skyscraper like the _____ ?
ROBERTO:	Yes. He has a great _____ of the city.

MACHIKO:	So, Roberto, what will you do in New York?
ROBERTO:	Well, I'm not very interested in shopping, but I want to go to the Metropolitan Museum. It says here that it's the most _____ museum in New York. I wonder if they have any Brazilian _____ .
MACHIKO:	Probably. It says here the museum has collections from all over the _____ . But I'd rather go shopping! There are lots of nice shops in New York, but you need a lot of _____ .

ROBERTO:	Another thing I want to do is to try some restaurants. I want to eat at one of the _____ restaurants in Little Italy.
MACHIKO:	And don't forget the Chinese restaurants!
ROBERTO:	Of course! After I eat so much, I'll get some exercise in Central Park if the weather is _____ . I wonder if it says anything about theaters in New York . . .

MACHIKO:	That reminds me! I'm meeting my roommate Sue and her friend at the Bayside Theater tonight to see a play. Would you like to come with us, Roberto?
ROBERTO:	Sure! Thanks, Machiko. What play are we going to see?
MACHIKO:	We're going to see *A Streetcar Named Desire*.

Answers:　Chinatown　~~far~~　time　Empire State Building
view　famous　art　world　money
Italian　nice

D Here is a whole page from *This Is New York*. Read it once quickly. Then look at the questions below. Then read the text more carefully and look at the pictures. Choose the best answer for each question.

ENTERTAINMENT

Broadway is famous for its theaters. One part of Broadway is sometimes called "The Great White Way." The lights from all the theaters and advertisements here are very bright. There are more than thirty theaters in this district.

Times Square is the center of the theater district. An important evening in Times Square is New Year's Eve — December 31st. Crowds of people stand in the Square and wait for midnight. At midnight, everyone shouts "Happy New Year!" to everyone else.

There are small theaters in other parts of New York. These are called *Off-Broadway* theaters. New and unusual plays are performed in these theaters.

Movie theaters are everywhere in New York. Magazines give the names and the times of the films.

Opera, ballet, and concerts are performed at *Lincoln Center*. The buildings are modern, and Chagall's paintings in the *Metropolitan Opera House* are very beautiful. Lincoln Center·is on Broadway at 64th Street.

The present *Madison Square Garden* was built in 1968. Many kinds of sports events take place there. Once a year, the biggest circus in the world comes there too.

1. The "Great White Way" is another name for
   a. a theater   b. Broadway   c. a shopping street
2. Crowds stand in Times Square and wait for midnight
   a. every night   b. whenever there is a new play
   c. on December 31
3. If you want to see unusual plays in New York, you go to
   a. Broadway   b. Lincoln Center
   c. Off-Broadway theaters

4. The Metropolitan Opera House is known for its

    a. ballet, concerts, and opera   b. location   c. restaurant

5. You can find movie theaters in New York

    a. in one special area   b. at Lincoln Center

    c. throughout the city

6. You can see a circus at Madison Square Garden

    a. every day of the week   b. once a year   c. on weekends

7. The pictures show

    a. shopping areas   b. theater districts   c. sports arenas

3   REVIEW

A   When you are reading a book or magazine about the subject *entertainment*, you can predict some of the words you will read.

Example: You probably will read these words: theaters, cinemas, sports.

              You probably won't read this word: kitchen.

Now look at the subjects listed below. For each subject, choose four words you would probably see if you were reading about that subject.

1. In a magazine about *theater*

    stage   actor   performance   waiter   audience

2. In a magazine about *sports*

    winner   loser   dance   race   athletics

3. In a magazine about *movies*

    actor   producer   director   maps   cinema

4. In a description of a *restaurant*

    tasty   sweet   delicious   scoreboard   expensive

5. In a book about *dance*

    to move   to step   to jump   to turn   to sightsee

6. In a *travel* brochure

    tickets   love   prices   fares   planes

7. In a guide to a *national park*

    lake   path   trees   bears   actress

8. In a book about *driving*

    quickly   grassy   dangerously   slowly   safely

9. In a *romance* novel about two young people

    to meet   to like   to love   to kiss   to rehearse

B   Look at the words you said you would not find for each subject. Put each one in the list where you *would* expect to find it.

4 SKILLS CHECK ✔

You have read these parts of a guide book   the cover
                                                   the contents
                                                   the introduction
                                                   excerpts
                                                   pictures

You have practiced   using clues to guess words
                      using other words to guess meaning
                      putting words into subject groups
                      answering multiple-choice questions

You have used these words and expressions:

author

chapter

clue

contents

cover

excerpt

introduction

predict

title

4 FICTION

1 READING

On their way to the theater, Roberto and Machiko went to a bookstore to each buy a book to read at home. Machiko bought a book called *The House on the Hill*.

Before reading parts of Machiko's book, look at the cover and at the first illustration. Now answer this question:

What do you think the book will be about?
crime
science fiction
love
horror
war

Now read Chapter 1.

Chapter 1

It was a beautiful summer evening. Paul was happy. No more exams. College was finished. Now he needed a job. He wanted to be a writer and work for a newspaper. But first he needed a rest.

It was hot in the house. There was no wind.

"I'll go for a walk," said Paul to himself. "I'll go down to the river."

Paul lived in a small town, and he was soon outside in the country. He walked near the river and watched the water birds.

Suddenly, he saw the girl. She was standing alone, looking into the water. She was young and very beautiful. She had long, dark hair, and she was wearing a pretty white dress.

Paul went up to her.

"Hello," he said. "What's your name?"

"I'm Maria," she said, and she smiled at him.

Paul and Maria talked for a long time. The sun went down. It was nearly dark.

"I must go home," said Maria.

"Where do you live?"

"In the big white house on the hill," said Maria. "Where do you live?"

"In the little brown house near the market," said Paul.

They laughed. But Paul was sad. The house on the hill was big and important. Maria was rich, and he was poor. And Paul was in love.

2 PRACTICE

A   *The House on the Hill* is a love story. Read the first page again. While you are reading, take notes on the **outline** of the story. The first note in each section has been done.

Outline

THE CHARACTERS

THE BOY

1. his name _Paul_

2. wants to be _____

3. money: rich/poor? _____

4. feelings: happy/sad?

    at the beginning _____

    at the end _____

    about the girl _____

THE GIRL

1. her name _Maria_

2. her age _____

3. money: rich/poor? _____

4. appearance _____

    her hair _____

    her dress _____

THE PLACE

1. Paul walks where? _Along the river_

2. Paul lives where (town/city/country)? _____

3. his house: size/color? _____

4. her house: size/color? _____

THE TIME

1. Time of year _Summer_

2. Time of day

    at the beginning of the story _____

    at the end of the excerpt _____

B   After you have finished reading, do not look back at the story, but use your notes to write a paragraph about the characters, the place, and the time.

C   Here is another excerpt from the book. Before you read this part, you need to know the following information:

Paul lives with his mother – a poor, kind woman.

Maria lives with her mother – a rich, unkind woman.

In this excerpt, Paul visits Maria's mother for the first time.

Now, read the excerpt. While you are reading, think about the following:

Maria's mother: What are her feelings about Paul?

Maria: What are her feelings about Paul?

Paul: What are his feelings about Maria and her mother?

Money: What role does it play in the story?

"So you want to marry my daughter?" the old woman said. Her voice was hard.

Paul looked at her bravely. "Yes," he said. "I love Maria and I want to marry her"

The old woman laughed.

"You! A poor student! No money, no father, nothing! My daughter will never marry you."

Paul said nothing. He looked at Maria. She did not look at him.

"I am poor now," he said. "but one day I'll be a famous writer."

The old woman laughed again. "No," she said. "My daughter is not for you. She is going to be married soon. You will never see her again."

D   After you have read the excerpt, try to predict how the story will end. Here are five different guesses about the ending of the story. Discuss each guess. Which guess do you think is the *least* likely ending? Which guess(es) are *possible* endings? Which do you think is the *most* likely ending?

1. Maria kills her mother.

2. Paul marries someone other than Maria.

3. Paul kills Maria's mother.

4. Paul and Maria get married.

5. Maria marries someone other than Paul.

3 READING

Roberto wanted to buy a best-selling novel called *Hotel*. There were two editions of the book in the bookstore. One edition was very difficult to read, but the other was shorter and easier. Roberto bought the simplified edition.

Here are excerpts from both editions of *Hotel*. Text A is easier than Text B. Before you read, you need to know the following information:

Hotel is a story about the St. Gregory Hotel, the largest hotel in New Orleans. There are several characters in the story. Warren Trent is the proud owner of the St. Gregory Hotel. Peter McDermott is the assistant manager. Curtis O'Keefe and Dodo are guests at the St. Gregory Hotel. O'Keefe owns many hotels himself, and he wants to own more. He is interested in buying the St. Gregory Hotel.

TEXT A: SIMPLIFIED VERSION

Title: Hotel

Author: Arthur Hailey

1   Curtis O'Keefe and Dodo had moved into their suites, and were now sitting in O'Keefe's living room. O'Keefe was studying a report about the St. Gregory from a folder marked *Confidential*.

5   Dodo, after looking over the basket of fruit that Peter McDermott had sent them, chose an apple and began to slice it.

The telephone rang, and O'Keefe answered it. It was Warren Trent, who welcomed O'Keefe to his hotel and

10   asked if everything was all right. After O'Keefe's friendly reply that they couldn't be more comfortable — not even in an O'Keefe hotel — Trent invited O'Keefe and Dodo to have dinner alone with him that evening.

"We would be happy to dine with you," replied

15   O'Keefe, politely accepting the invitation. "And I do like your hotel very much," he added.

"I was afraid you would," remarked Trent.

O'Keefe laughed loudly. "We'll talk tonight, Warren," he said. "Perhaps we will discuss a little business, but

20   I'm mostly just looking forward to a talk with a great hotel man."

As O'Keefe hung up the telephone, Dodo frowned and asked, "If he's such a great hotel man, Curtis, why is he selling his hotel to you?"

While you are reading, try to understand all of Text A, but do not try to understand all of Text B. Both texts describe a telephone conversation that O'Keefe has after he and Dodo arrive at the St. Gregory.

After you have read the excerpts, do the exercises that follow them.

TEXT B: ORIGINAL VERSION

Title: Hotel

Author: Arthur Hailey

1   Curtis O'Keefe and Dodo had settled comfortably into their communicating suites, with Dodo unpacking for both of them as she always enjoyed doing. Now, in the larger of the two living rooms, the hotelier was
5   studying a financial statement, one of several in a blue folder labeled *Confidential — St. Gregory, preliminary survey.*

Dodo, after a careful inspection of the magnificent basket of fruit which Peter McDermott had ordered
10   delivered to the suite, selected an apple and was slicing it as the telephone at O'Keefe's elbow rang twice within a few minutes.

The first call was from Warren Trent — a polite welcome and an inquiry seeking assurance that
15   everything was in order. After a genial acknowledgment that it was — "Couldn't be better, my dear Warren, even in an O'Keefe hotel" — Curtis O'Keefe accepted an invitation for himself and Dodo to dine privately with the St. Gregory's proprietor that evening.

20   "We'll be truly delighted," the hotelier affirmed graciously, "and, by the way, I admire your house."

"That," Warren Trent said drily down the telephone, "is what I've been afraid of."

O'Keefe guffawed. "We'll talk tonight, Warren. A
25   little business if we must, but mostly I'm looking forward to a conversation with a great hotel man."

As he replaced the telephone Dodo's brow was furrowed. "If he's such a great hotel man, Curtis, why's he selling out to you?"

4 PRACTICE

A Taking notes. Complete these notes about this part of the story.

Title: _____   Author: _____

Name of hotel: _____

Owner of hotel: _____

Hotel guests: _____

O'Keefe owns: _____

O'Keefe wants to buy: _____

What did Peter McDermott send to the suite? _____

B Comparing. The chart below has words from Text A and Text B. For each word or phrase given there is a word or phrase with a similar meaning in the other text. Find the missing words and write them in the blanks. The line numbers are given to help you find the words. The first one has been done for you.

TEXT A

report _____ (3)

looking over (5)

_____ (6)

friendly reply (11)

have dinner (13)

_____ (13)

politely (15)

laughed loudly (18)

_____ (20)

_____ (22)

TEXT B

financial statement   (5)

_____ (8)

selected (10)

_____ (15)

_____ (18)

privately (18)

_____ (21)

_____ (24)

conversation (26)

Dodo's brow was furrowed (27)

Which text is longer?

Which text is easier? Why?

5 REVIEW

Making a summary. Choose a book you have read recently and make a record of it like this:

Author: _____   Title: _____

Summary

> Was it long/short? Was it easy/difficult?
> What kind of book was it? fiction/nonfiction?
> What was it about? Discuss subject/characters/place/time/events.
> Did you like it?
> Would you recommend this book to your friends?
> Would you read any more books by the same author or on the same topic?

6 SKILLS CHECK ✔

You have read	excerpts from a story
	excerpts from a novel
	an outline

You have practiced	making predictions before you read
	taking notes while you read
	comparing texts after you have read them
	summarizing a story

You have used these words and expressions:

author
character
edition
events
guess
notes
novel
opinion
prediction
subject
summary
text
title

5 A THEATER VISIT

1 READING

Roberto and Machiko met Sue and her friend Peter at the theater. They were going to a **play** called *A Streetcar Named Desire* by Tennessee Williams. Machiko introduced Roberto to Sue and Peter. Then there was just enough time for a drink before the play started. Sue and Peter went to order the drinks, while Roberto and Machiko read a theater **program** about the play.

2 PRACTICE

Study the excerpts from the theater program for *A Streetcar Named Desire* and complete the exercises.

A About the theatre

The Bayside Theater

The Bayside Theater opened under the management of J. B. Iverson on October 15, 1935, with the comedy *Jubilee*, starring Agnes Miller and Robert Sampson. After 108 performances of *Jubilee*, the theater began playing a very different type of entertainment with *Damaged Goods*, whose first public performances in this country took place here.

EXERCISE

Answer true or false to these statements about the theater.

The Bayside Theater opened in the 1940s.

The first show at the Bayside Theater was *Jubilee*.

Jubilee had fewer than 100 performances.

The first manager of the Bayside Theater was J.B. Iverson.

Damaged Goods was a comedy.

B About the play

> ... *A Streetcar Named Desire* was first performed at the Barrymore Theater in New York on December 3, 1947. It was directed by Elia Kazan, and starred Marlon Brando as Stanley Kowalski, Kim Hunter as Stella, and Jessica Tandy as Blanche DuBois...
>
> ...The play takes place in the spring, summer, and early fall in New Orleans...
>
> ...There will be two 15-minute intermissions, after Scene 4 and Scene 6.

EXERCISE

Answer yes or no to these questions about the play.

Was *A Streetcar Named Desire* playing in 1946?

Does the play take place in New York?

Does the action of the play take place within one year?

Did Elia Kazan star as Stanley Kowalski in the first performance of the play?

Was the first performance of *A Streetcar Named Desire* over forty years ago?

C About the author

> Tennessee Williams was born in Columbus, Mississippi, on March 26, 1911. He worked for many years without critical recognition and finally received the Drama Critics' Circle Award for his play *The Glass Menagerie*, which he wrote in 1945. He wrote *A Streetcar Named Desire* in 1947. Some of his other highly acclaimed works are *Cat on a Hot Tin Roof*, *The Rose Tattoo*, *Suddenly Last Summer*, and *The Night of the Iguana*. Today he is considered one of the outstanding American playwrights. Tennessee Williams died on February 25, 1983.

EXERCISE

Fill in the blanks about the author.

Tennessee Williams was born in _____ .

He received the Drama Critics' Circle Award for his play _____ , which he wrote in _____ .

He wrote _____ in 1947.

Tennessee Williams died on _____ .

D About the actors

A Streetcar Named Desire
by
Tennessee Williams

————— // —————

Characters in order of their appearance

Negro Woman	Lisa Jackson
Eunice Hubbell	Judith Pike
Stanley Kowalski	Tony Anderson
Stella Kowalski	Carol Brown
Steve Hubbell	Robert Walker
Harold Mitchell (Mitch)	Larry Jones
Mexican Woman	Maria Lopez
Blanche DuBois	Nancy Winter
Pablo Gonzales	Carlos Gomez
A Young Collector	George Smith
Nurse	Ann New
Doctor	Paul Murphy

EXERCISE

Give the right information about the actors.

How many characters are there in *A Streetcar Named Desire*?

Which character is the actress Carol Brown playing?

Which character is Nancy Winter playing?

Who is playing the part of Mitch?

Who is playing the part of the nurse?

E About what to do after the show

EXERCISE

Choose the best answers.

a. The Bay Window Restaurant is

    a bar

    a restaurant

    a theater

b. You can order dinner at the
Bay Window Restaurant

    on weeknights

    every night

    on weekends

c. Bay Window Restaurant
advertises

    seafood only

    meat dishes only

    both seafood and meat
    dishes

Bay Window RESTAURANT

Live Maine Lobster / Fresh Fish
Steaks & Chops
Cocktails • Dinner Nightly

2040 Broadway, San Francisco
Next to Bayside Theater • Reservations (415) 555-1855
Valet Pkg.

d. Bay Window Restaurant is next to

> the Paramount Theater
> the Bayside Theater
> Bay View Community College

e. Bay Window Restaurant's telephone number is advertised so you can

> order dinner
> arrange for parking
> make reservations

3 REVIEW

Roberto, Machiko, Sue, and Peter all enjoyed *A Streetcar Named Desire* very much. As they were leaving the theater, Sue told them she had four tickets for another play, *Death of a Salesman*, by Arthur Miller. The four friends decided they would all go.

Complete their conversations at the theater.

A Finding seats.

ROBERTO:	It looks like we've got great seats.
PETER:	Yeah. We're in the orchestra, section 3. What row are we in?
ROBERTO:	The ticket says Row _____ .
PETER:	OK. It's down here. What seat number do you have?
ROBERTO:	Seat _____ .

B Reading about Arthur Miller in the program.

Arthur Miller —
A Short Biography

1915	Born in New York City.
1936	Attended University of Michigan. Studied journalism and began to write plays.
1940	Married Mary Slattery.
1947	The play *All My Sons* was produced. Won New York Drama Critics' Circle Award.
1949	Wrote *Death of a Salesman*, which won the Pulitzer Prize.
1953	Wrote *The Crucible*.
1956	Married movie actress Marilyn Monroe.
1961	Wrote screenplay of *The Misfits*, starring Marilyn Monroe.
1962	Married photographer Inge Morath.
1964 —	Continues to write fiction, articles, and plays. *Death of a Salesman* and *The Crucible* have both been produced on television.

SUE: I didn't know Arthur Miller was _____ to Marilyn
            Monroe.

PETER: I knew that, but I didn't know she starred in the
            _____ , and that Miller wrote
            the _____ for her.

MACHIKO: Look at this list of Miller's works. _____
            was only the second play he wrote.

ROBERTO: Yes. And he's also written screenplays and _____ .

Works by
Arthur Miller

Plays

1947	All My Sons
1949	Death of a Salesman
1953	The Crucible
1955	A View from the Bridge
1964	After the Fall
1964	Incident at Vichy
1968	The Price
1972	The Creation of the World and Other Business

Screenplays

1961	The Misfits
1980	Playing for Time

Fiction

1973	Focus
1967	I Don't Need You Anymore

C Looking at part of a scene from *Death of a Salesman*.

> BIFF: Shake hands, Dad.
> WILLY: Not my hand.
> BIFF: I was hoping not to go this way.
> WILLY: Well, this is the way you're going. Good-by.
> *Biff looks at him a moment, then turns sharply and goes to the stairs.*
> WILLY, *stops him with*: May you rot in hell if you leave this house!
> BIFF, *turning*: Exactly what is it that you want from me?
> WILLY: I want you to know, on the train, in the mountains, in the valleys, wherever you go, that you cut down your life for spite!
> BIFF: No, no.
> WILLY: Spite, spite, is the word of your undoing! And when you're down and out, remember what did it. When you're rotting somewhere beside the railroad tracks, remember, and don't you dare blame it on me!
> BIFF: I'm not blaming it on you!
> WILLY: I won't take the rap for this, you hear?

MACHIKO: I think Biff is Willy's _____ .

ROBERTO: Why doesn't Willy want Biff to _____ ?

MACHIKO: I guess we'll find out why. The lights are going out – the play is starting!

4 SKILLS CHECK ✔

You have read excerpts from	a theater program
	a play
You have practiced	reading for information
	reading for meaning
	reading for pleasure

You have used these words and expressions:

actors
intermission
play
program
reservations
screenplay
show
theater

Reading Review Three

1 REASONS FOR READING: **What** People Read

A Study these pictures of people and the different magazines they read. Think about the people, about their lives, and their interests. Then use the pictures to help you complete the exercises.

B Read this paragraph about *Jack and Jill* magazine and its readers. Then look at the missing words and their meanings.

Jack and Jill is usually bought by adults for children. It is a magazine for both (1) . . . and girls. Many children start reading *Jack and Jill* from the age of five. Many of them read it for three or four years, up to the (2) . . . of eight or nine. Most *Jack and Jill* readers live in (3) . . . areas like Bay View, but the magazine is enjoyed all over the country. *Jack and Jill* is not expensive and it is read by children from every (4) . . . group.

Study the missing words and their meanings:

1. *Jack and Jill* is a magazine for both *boys and girls.*

2. Many of them read *Jack and Jill* for three or four years, up to the *age of eight or nine.*

3. Most *Jack and Jill* readers live in *suburban areas* like Bay View.

4. *Jack and Jill* is not expensive and it is read by children from every *income group.*

C Now guess the missing words from these four paragraphs.

Seventeen is for _____ . Most of them are _____ . They live in all _____ of the country. Girls from all income groups read *Seventeen*, but the price indicates that this magazine is probably most popular with girls from middle to upper-middle class _____ .

Town and Country is read by men and _____ . This magazine is mainly popular with middle-_____ people. As the title of the magazine suggests, many of its readers live in _____ and in the _____ . The magazine is read by people who are interested in art, architecture, fashion, and food. Many of *Town and Country*'s readers have above-_____ incomes.

Popular Photography is read by both women and _____ . They are from all age _____ , but the magazine is most popular with readers in their twenties and thirties. Because _____ is an expensive hobby, it is not surprising that many readers of *Popular Photography* are from average and _____ -income groups.

Parents is designed for both men and women, but it is more often read by mothers than by _____ . *Parents* readers have children of all _____ , but it is read most by women who are expecting their first child. The magazine sells well in urban areas. It is read in _____ and cities all over the United States. It is bought by _____ income groups, but mostly by average and above-average income groups.

2   REASONS FOR READING: Why People Read

A   This page contains background information about some readers. Read it quickly but carefully.

Jane is in her forties. She is a bank teller. Her husband likes gardening books. Her children read about history and geography. But Jane likes more exciting books, although she doesn't get much time to read them.

Dave is twenty-two. He works in an electronics factory. He enjoys reading about his hobby in his spare time.

Ann is seventeen. She is in high school. She has to study French and German. She likes these subjects, but she finds them difficult.

Bob is over seventy. When he was a truck driver, he saw a lot of small towns in his state. Now he is not working and has time to study their history.

Lisa and Mark are students at a community college. Lisa is studying fashion design. Mark is studying English literature, but he wants to be a musician.

B Now look at what the following chart tells you about each person. Use the background information and the chart to help you do the exercises as quickly as you can.

WHO (readers)	WHAT (text types)	WHY (reasons for reading)	WHEN (time)	WHERE (place)
Jane	Science fiction stories. Magazines and comics.	Pleasure. Excitement. Escape to another world.	Any time she can find.	On her way to work. At home.
Dave	Anything about baseball.	Relaxation. Interest.	Evenings. Weekends.	At home.
Ann	Nonfiction books about France and Germany – especially dictionaries.	Information. Help with her schoolwork.	Days, evenings. Not weekends.	At home. At school. At the library.
Bob	Old maps and guides about small towns.	Information. Pleasure. To find new places.	Any time.	At home. Places he visits.
Lisa and Mark	Fashion magazines. Rock music magazines.	Interest. Enjoyment. New ideas. To find jobs!	Lisa–all the time. Mark–when not studying.	At home. At college. In class!

And what about you?

_____

C True or false?

    1. Jane likes reading gardening books.

    2. Dave reads about his hobby in the evenings and on weekends.

    3. Ann uses dictionaries to help her with her schoolwork.

    4. Bob only likes to read old maps at home.

    5. Lisa and Mark like to read books connected with their studies.

D Rearrange the words to make complete sentences.

    1. doesn't   connected   his   with   job   books
        Dave   read

    2. Bob   his   uses   maps   in   to   old   state
        the   towns   study

    3. them   advertisements   with   Lisa   magazines
        Mark   and   in   read   jobs   about

    4. children   Jane's   like   husband   science fiction
        and   don't   stories

    5. nonfiction   lot   French   Ann   German   and
        a   uses   books   about   of

E Choose the best answers.

    1. _____ has lots of time to read what he wants.
      a. Mark
      b. Bob
      c. Dave

    2. For her schoolwork, Ann must use
      a. recipes.
      b. timetables.
      c. dictionaries.

    3. Bob reads old maps because
      a. he's a historian.
      b. he's a truck driver.
      c. he's interested in the history of small towns.

    4. Jane reads science fiction
      a. at work.
      b. in her spare time.
      c. on weekends only.

    5. Mark reads rock music magazines
      a. at school only.
      b. at home only.
      c. anywhere.

F Read the whole paragraph. Then guess the missing words.

_____ do people read? For a variety of reasons. Some for pleasure, others because they have to. And _____ do people read? Well, some people don't read very often, but others read all the time, day and night. And _____ ? The answer is simple – anywhere and everywhere. But the most important question is_____ do people read? Advertisements? Stories? Science books? Maps? It could be anything! Ask your family and friends all these questions. Then make your own _____ of who reads what, why, when, and where!

INTRODUCTION TO THE IDEAS BEHIND THE CONTENT AND ORGANIZATION OF THE COURSE

Reading as part of the language learning process

Task Reading is intended for students who have mastered some basic structures and vocabulary in English but are still at an elementary to low-intermediate level.

Successful and well-directed reading for students at this early stage in foreign language learning can be important in developing self-confidence and new motivation. This is especially so if, at the beginning of the learning process, the support of the printed word has been removed. The introduction of the activity of reading, which is common to all *other* subjects in the curriculum, gives students the opportunity to use skills and strategies they already possess in their own language and to apply them to English.

When reading in the new language, students can begin to see how the grammar and vocabulary they are learning are used in the communication of information and ideas. They can also be exposed to new and unfamiliar language that is within their receptive and predictive range but beyond their productive ability. More importantly perhaps, reading, which is a very individual and self-directed process, allows students to see for themselves, often independently of the teacher, how the English language realizes the functions and purposes they are familiar with on their own.

Reading as communication

Most modern courses in English as a second or foreign language offer teachers a communicative syllabus, which gives as much importance to the functional uses of the language as to its linguistic forms. This book aims to support and complement such courses, by recognizing reading as a communicative rather than a passive activity. But developing real communicative ability in a foreign language, and being an active reader of it, requires from the learner more awareness and consciousness of learning strategies than does reading in the native language. *Task Reading* therefore, emphasizes these approaches to reading in a foreign language:

1. Transfer of reading skills from the native language to English.
2. The use of authentic or realistic source texts.
3. Pre-text orientation, especially the identification of reader and writer intent.
4. Identification of functional aspects of written discourse.
5. Integration of reading with speaking, writing, and study skills.

1. *Transfer of reading skills*

An important aim of this course is to activate the "unconscious" skills possessed in relation to the native language and demonstrate how these can be consciously applied to English. All too often a foreign language is taught in isolation from the rest of the learning curriculum or from the content and context of the student's real motivation for learning it. Lower-level students are, in addition, at a unique disadvantage in the language classroom, since they are "back at the beginning," whatever their age or status. Unfortunately, too, there is much in the theory and methodology of language teaching developed over the past decades that disregards the learners' existing range of study skills, most particularly those relating to the language they have already mastered – their native language.

When reading in their own language, most students know why they are reading a text, or they bring some knowledge or interest of their own to it. Before starting to read they survey the whole text and identify features that give them clues to type, function, and style. Fluent readers then read in broad phrases, skip words or constructions that don't obstruct total phrase meaning, and unconsciously employ skills like collocation and prediction for guessing meaning from context. They also confidently ignore large parts of a text when directed to extract specific facts or ideas.

But many of the same students fail to apply these strategies to texts in English, for a variety of reasons. The text looks unfamiliar, they come to it "cold," they lack extra-textual information such as time, setting, cultural environment – all of which affects their usual reading strategy. As a result, they lack confidence and revert to a linear approach to reading, with frequent recourse to glossary or dictionary.

Task Reading is particularly directed at helping such students to be more aware and self-conscious in their use of reading skills, and to apply them directly to their work in the English language classroom. In this way, students can increase their general language awareness, and foreign language teachers can make their contribution to general study skills development within the whole learning curriculum.

2. *Use of authentic or realistic source texts*

In spoken communication, meaning is aided by nonverbal means, such as gesture and posture. These paralinguistic features also exist in written communication, and awareness and recognition of them is tremendously useful in activating the predictive abilities of foreign language readers. Much of this first book is, therefore, directed at the recognition, analysis, and interpretation of such features in English texts.

To accomplish this, the texts themselves must be realistic, and there must be a realistic interpretation of what constitutes a "text." Many teachers think of a "text" as a piece of continuous prose; and many textbook writers, conscious of this, offer "simplified" texts based on the known speaking and hearing vocabulary of the intended students. It is questionable whether such texts are really simpler for the reader. Certainly they are not realistic. Crucially they lack any of the paralinguistic features that give readers such useful signals to meaning.

Information and ideas are often carried by means other than continuous prose. For example, in the first unit of the Student's Book, the same biographical information is presented both as prose and as entries on a record card, and the students are directed to transfer the information from one mode to the other. Most textbooks today are full of nonverbal devices, such as maps, charts, tables, drawings, and symbols, which supplement or replace the verbal message. These are "texts" in their own right — they carry meaning; and aspects of them can sometimes be language or culture specific (such as abbreviations). Familiarity with these nonverbal devices can aid the fluency of all students, and is vital for those students who will go on to use English for more specific purposes.

All students can absorb (or ignore) language beyond their productive range if they are confident and have a specific purpose in mind. In *Task Reading*, we have tried to balance sensitivity to the students' elementary language level with the challenge of exposing them to a wide range of "real" text sources. This has been done by paying special attention to pre-text orientation, and through setting comprehension *tasks* rather than comprehension *questions* – tasks that are designed to help the reader approach a text with a purpose in mind.

3. Pre-text work

When reading an unfamiliar text, there are three broad stages: recognition, decoding, and interpretation. It is the "recognition" phase that often presents the most difficulty when reading in a foreign language, and it is the one that is often most neglected. However, this pre-reading stage is vitally important and activates the students' expectations and predictive ability.

Therefore *Task Reading* puts its main emphasis on this important part of the overall reading process. Students do not approach a text without first establishing purpose, both their own and the writer's; and texts are not presented in isolation from a situational or functional context.

Throughout the book, students are helped to acquire techniques for previewing a whole text by "window shopping" for clues to type, function, and style. They are also given explicit guidance on what these clues are, from visual and typographical features to persuasive use of language.

The role of the teacher in helping students to establish a reading strategy appropriate to a particular text type, and in helping them to define their purpose in reading it, is clearly vital, and guidance is given in the more detailed methodological suggestions that follow.

4. Identification of functional aspects of written discourse

The previous section discussed the importance of using whole text features as an aid to comprehension. *Task Reading* pays special attention to the recognition and interpretation of *nonlinguistic* (illustration, typography, etc.) and *paralinguistic* (punctuation, emphasis signals, etc.) features, where they relate to readers' expectations and are signposts to meaning.

We have also said that reading is not a passive language skill but a communicative one. By this we mean that in any piece of writing (whether a timetable or a piece of narrative prose) there is a hidden conversation between writer and reader. The writer has certain intentions (to inform, to instruct, to persuade, to amuse), and chooses an appropriate format and *language* to achieve the communicative intent. The writer takes account of the reader's unheard response, anticipates unspoken questions, and structures the discourse and chooses words accordingly.

Task Reading, therefore, is also concerned with raising students' awareness of specific *linguistic* features as clues to meaning, and with the relationship of these to function and style. This is particularly so in Part Two, where units are organized under such functional categories as *Instruction, Opinion, Persuasion*. Throughout the book, specific text types and verbal devices are clearly identified for students in terms of their purpose, and students are given practice in recognizing and describing their function. In order to help them apply these insights to other related texts, students are given a basic vocabulary for describing the relationship between form and function. The *Skills Check* at the end of each unit is designed to help students to do this.

5. Integration of reading with speaking, writing, and study skills

Many English language textbooks contain separate sections on oral work, on comprehension, and on composition, sometimes linked by theme or topic. But *reading* as a skill is often taken for granted or given a subsidiary role.

This text, however, is not about reading as a *separate* skill. It is concerned with the relationship between the skills, particularly the transition between the learner's receptive and productive abilities, and the transfer of information from a nonverbal to a verbal mode. Many activities in this book, therefore, are designed to integrate specific reading skills with related skills in speaking or writing, in a communicative situation.

For these reasons, the approach to "reading comprehension questions" is somewhat different in this text. Exercises start from the premise that "it is not a normal communicative activity to answer questions about what we have read, but to *do* or *say* something as a result of having read it."[1] So this book does not follow the traditional pattern of text followed by comprehension questions used as testing devices. It is more concerned with

[1] H. Widdowson, *Teaching Language as Communication* (Oxford University Press, 1978), p. 5.

giving the reader techniques for getting into the text and using what is extracted in a communicative way.

Ideally, reading in the foreign language should contribute to the development of the students' general reading ability. This is better achieved through questions that direct the learners' attention to what is going on in the text or in their own mind, than by those that test their ability to "compose" an answer.

Summary

Task Reading, therefore, focuses on the nature of texts and people's reasons for writing or reading them – the What, Why, and How of pre-reading and reading.

Exercises and activities are as various as the text types to which they relate. They are devised to help students to orient themselves to the text setting, to survey and predict from the whole text rather than tackle it in a linear way, and to identify textual clues of a nonlinguistic, paralinguistic, and linguistic nature. They include *pre-reading* activities such as matching and word play; *identification* activities directed at type, function, and style; *reviewing* activities, including skimming, scanning, and prediction; and *composition* activities involving the active use of study skills, such as information transfer or oral and written composition. Traditional questioning devices, such as Yes/No, True/False, Multiple-choice, and Completion, are included but are introduced as useful techniques for the student to master, rather than as ends in themselves. *Task Reading* helps students to activate and refine their content and cultural *schemata*: that is, their "frames of reference," which, as individuals, readers, and learners, they bring to the reading of English as a foreign or second language.[2]

CONTENTS OF *TASK READING*

The storyline

There is a continuing story in *Task Reading*, which follows the activities of Machiko and Roberto, two college students in the San Francisco Bay Area. This has three purposes:

1. To give overall unity to the material.
2. To provide characters and situations with which students can identify.
3. To provide functional and situational settings for the reading texts.

Each unit begins with a short narrative or dialogue on the activities of the two students in the story, to which the focal reading text is related.

The parts

There are three parts in the book:

1. **Reading for Information** – where the focus is on topic and typography.
2. **Reading for Meaning** – where the focus is on function and form
3. **Reading for Pleasure** – where the focus is on text and mode (type of reading).

At the end of each part there is a *Reading Review* — to review, consolidate, and extend the work done in that part.

The units

Each part contains five units. Each unit begins with a presentation of the learning focus, which is usually a piece of printed realia needed and used by the characters in the story. Students then begin to interact with this text in a variety of ways designed to highlight and analyze its special features.

Students next practice the application of these reading strategies to other, related texts. They are then ready for the *Skills Check*, which summarizes the text types they have used and the skills they have practiced.

The artwork

There is a wide variety of visual material in *Task Reading*, none of which exists for purely illustrative (or decorative!) reasons. The photographs, drawings, and printed realia are always an integral part of the text to which they relate. They have been designed to present important typographical features, or as an essential part of the understanding of the whole text. It is important to the methodology of this course that these be used actively by students in the development of their overall comprehension strategy.

How to use *Task Reading*

In using this book, the teacher's overall strategy will include the following elements:

1. Pre-text work
2. Presentation
3. Analysis, Extraction, and Transference
4. Checking of learning

These elements have been built into the structure of the material in the Student's Book, but the order and weighting will be subject to such variables as teacher and learner preference, teaching situation, and the particular nature of each unit of work.

---

[2] See, for example, P. Carrell, "Content and Formal Schemata in ESL Reading," *TESOL Quarterly*, vol. 261, no. 3 (1987).

1. Pre-text work

The reader's orientation to a text as well as intelligent guessing are important elements in the reading process. Teachers should, therefore, do everything possible to activate these in approaching each new unit of work. In order to stimulate interest and introduce the vocabulary and themes in each unit, prereading activities are essential. Such activities include:

- Asking students about experiences they have had that relate to the theme of the unit.
- Supplying any necessary cultural information.
- Vocabulary brainstorming.
- Predicting outcomes.
- Bringing in related newspaper/magazine articles, audio- or videotapes, pictures or photos to describe and generate interest. These can also be used later in the unit for any extension work.

2. Presentation

The presentation of the opening text in each unit should vary according to its nature. Ideally, it will always involve elements of some or all of these:

(a) Previewing – for type, function, and style.
(b) Prediction – of content and purpose.
(c) Recognition – of semantic features and paralinguistic clues.
(d) Establishing a reading strategy appropriate to that text and its functional setting.

A recommended method of presenting the Reading in each unit is given in the *Unit Notes* that follow, although these are not intended to be prescriptive in any way.
The suggestions made include:

1. Scanning to predict story or setting.
2. Skimming to identify key features.
3. Teacher reading aloud.
4. Students reading silently.
5. Students reading in pairs.
6. Reading parts of the text in relation to other printed realia.
7. The use of recorded material.

3. Analysis, extraction, and transference

The activities of analysis, extraction, and transference are to a large extent built into the structure of the exercise material. It is essential when using this book not to "overteach" but to act as a guide to your students, giving them space to think, work, and discover for themselves. For this reason, the first exercises in each unit have been designed to provide a reading strategy in themselves, usually with one example to discuss with the teacher so that your students know what to do. The *Unit Notes* that follow make suggestions about which exercises can be done with the teacher, or in student pairs, or individually. This will free you to work with individuals or groups, encouraging your students to be aware of, discuss with you, and describe their own learning strategies.

The *Unit Notes* also make suggestions about further transference and extension work that might involve preparation of additional material yourself. It is desirable to have available in your classroom some reference books in English, such as an atlas, a dictionary, a biographical encyclopedia. In order to prepare further work of the kind students have found enjoyable and useful in the book, a supply of English magazines, newspapers, and simplified readers will also be useful.

4. Learning checks

Two learning checks are provided in the Student's Book: the *Skills Check* at the end of each unit and the *Reading Review* at the end of each part. These are not intended as tests, but as means of organizing and applying what the students are learning. The *Skills Check* encourages a practical approach to reading skills in a second language by:

(a) Identifying a range of text types related to each topic.
(b) Training students to recognize and describe their function.
(c) Labeling the microskills used.
(d) Listing vocabulary words and expressions used in the unit.

The first part of the *Skills Check* ("You have read...") summarizes the text types handled in the unit and builds a cumulative "reading vocabulary" for students. The second part ("You have practiced...") lists reading features. You can give further practice if this seems necessary. The third part lists words and expressions used in the unit. Encourage students to keep a vocabulary notebook in which they record words and definitions from the unit that they want to remember or have trouble remembering. This can be done as homework. They should update their notebooks regularly, and also enter related words that they find on their own.

The *Reading Review* is designed to review and integrate the work in progress, and to develop the students' confidence and motivation. Both of these learning checks also provide you with material for testing, as well as ideas for the preparation of further similar material for practice.

PART ONE: Reading for Information

Unit 1   People

SKILLS COVERED

- Extracting information from prose, forms, letters, and charts.

- Transferring information from one mode to another.

1   READING

A Have students look at the photo of Machiko Morita. Encourage them to make predictions about the reading passage (the description of Machiko) by discussing the photo (e.g., Machiko's age, where she is from, her appearance). Then have students read the description of Machiko silently. When they are finished, have them discuss whether their predictions about her were correct.

B Have students look at the title of the form. Ask them about forms they have filled out that were similar to this one. Check students' comprehension of terms and expressions, such as "department store," "marital status," "present title." Have students finish reading the form silently.

C Point out the format and style of Roberto's letter before having students read the content. Ask students who the letter is for, who wrote it, and where the letter writer is from. Have them describe the purpose and content of any business-type letters they have written or received recently. Then have students read the body of the letter.

2   PRACTICE

A Divide the class into pairs or small groups. Have them answer the questions orally or in writing, and give help when needed. If their answers are written, check answers orally.

B As a class, brainstorm information about Sue, writing students' ideas on the board. Reread the description of Machiko and go over the organization of the description with the students. Then have students work in pairs and write a description of Sue. Give help when needed. Have one or two of the stronger students write their descriptions on the board.

C Have students work alone. Check their answers orally.

D (*Note*: You may want to make copies of the Student Record Card ahead of time to distribute in class.) Have students complete the form for themselves. Then have them exchange the form with a partner and write a description like the one they did of Sue Brown in Practice B. Ask a few volunteers to read their descriptions aloud.

E Have students circulate and interview each other in order to complete the chart. If the class is at a lower level, write the interview questions ("What is your name?" "What country are you from?") on the board and have the students practice them before beginning.

3   REVIEW

Introduce this activity with a brief discussion about hobbies, sports, and majors. Make sure students understand the vocabulary in the descriptions. Have them fill in the chart with a partner. Check answers orally.

4   SKILLS CHECK

Have students identify at least one example of each reading type and one example of each skill in the unit. (An example of a *description* is the paragraph about Machiko at the beginning of the unit. Students practiced the skill of *filling in a chart* when they completed the Class Information Chart.)

Have students say the vocabulary aloud. Check their comprehension. Students can begin a vocabulary notebook in which they record new words and expressions from the *Skills Check* section of each unit. Encourage students to add words to their vocabulary lists outside of class as well.

Unit 2   Places

SKILLS COVERED

- Using alphabetical indexes and keys to determine place/distance/conditions.

- Using grid references to find location and scales to determine distances.

- Transferring information to speech or writing by giving full lexical value to abbreviations.

1 READING

- Ask students about times they have had to ask for directions or follow a map. Bring in a campus or town map to display while working on this unit.

- Remind students of the storyline and that Machiko is going to start studying English.

- Have students read the dialogue between Machiko and Sue silently. Then select two students to read the conversation aloud.

- Divide the class into pairs and have students substitute local street names in the dialogue, using the map you have brought in.

2 PRACTICE

A First, do the example with the class orally. Then divide students into small groups to locate the rest of the streets. Check answers orally.

B Go over the key with the class. Check their understanding and pronunciation, and make sure they can handle it easily. Then do the example with the class. Have students work in pairs to complete the exercise. Check answers orally.

C Have students do this exercise alone.

D Demonstrate how to use the scale of miles. As a class, measure a few sample distances (e.g., the distance from the Chamber of Commerce to the intersection of Spring Way and Mission Boulevard, or the distance from Sue's apartment to the train station), using the sample phrases supplied in the student text. Then have students complete the activity in pairs.

E–F Present the grid map of the United States and southern Canada. Is your city represented? If not, have students add it! Have students complete the exercises in pairs or in small groups.

G Introduce abbreviations by explaining their function (to take up less space) and selecting two states for examples (e.g., Georgia: GA; Maryland: MD). Have students do the exercise individually, then choose students to write answers on the board. Let the other students direct those at the board to make corrections and fill in any missing information.

H Have students do this exercise alone or as homework.

3 REVIEW

Introduce this section with a brief discussion about weather and weather reports. Bring in weather reports from local newspapers and discuss what kinds of information they contain and how to find information quickly. Ask questions such as "What's the weather like today?" "What will the weather be like for the next few days?" "What's the weather like in the city you come from?" "What's the weather like in [name some major cities]?"

A Present the weather report in the student text. Have students quickly scan it to locate the map, area forecasts, index, key, and chart. Discuss the purpose of each of these. Ask students questions such as "Which area is our city in?" "What weather is forecast for our area?" "What cities are in Area 4?" "What is the temperature in Lima?" "What is the weather like in Tokyo?" As a class, identify what country each city in the World Weather Chart belongs to.

B Do the examples as a class. If students are having difficulty, do more examples. Then allow students to proceed in pairs or in small groups, encouraging them to extend their conversations if possible.

Unit 3   Directions

SKILLS COVERED

- Recognizing and reading words, symbols, diagrams, and abbreviations used in giving directions.

- Using scales and keys to interpret information on maps and plans.

- Transferring information from maps, charts, plans, and diagrams to written or spoken English.

1 READING

- Have students look at the photos and try to predict the story. Then have them read the dialogue to check their predictions.

- Ask if anyone in the class has ever gotten lost. Have a few students describe their experiences.

- Choose two students to read the dialogue aloud, using appropriate intonation. If they need more work with this, repeat the exercise with students in small groups.

2 PRACTICE

A (*Note*: You may want to make extra copies of the map before class.) Present the map and discuss its features (compass, street names, abbreviations, etc.). Read Sue's instructions aloud and have students trace her directions on the map. Then read the passage about Machiko aloud and have students trace her mistakes. Discuss what mistake Machiko made.

B Have students do this exercise individually.

C Provide an example for students by drawing a map from one part of the campus to another. Have students work silently drawing their maps and writing their instructions. Then have them work in pairs, with one student reading his or her written directions while the other traces the directions on the map.

D Ask students what they know about the state of Texas. Then present the map of Texas. Review directional vocabulary (north, south, southwest, etc.). Do this exercise orally first, then have students write out the answers.

E Model the question-answer example, then give students three minutes to complete the list.

3   REVIEW

A Ask students if they have visited a local museum. What did they like best? Read the message from Sue aloud while students trace the directions on the floor plan. Point out the use of room numbers and symbols for identification.

B First, have students practice the directional phrases listed in their book. Then they can either write their instructions alone or give them orally in small groups.

Unit 4   Journeys

SKILLS COVERED

- Using nonalphabetical keys to get information about travel.

- Decoding symbols and converting them to words.

- Using letters and symbols to guess meaning from context.

1 READING

Preview the storyline. (Sue went to the museum on the subway to meet Peter.) Have students describe their own experiences on rapid transit systems. If possible, bring in maps or guides from other systems.

A Familiarize the students with the BART map. Practice saying the names of stations and lines. Explain what a transfer station is. Ask questions such as "Which trains stop at the Fruitvale Station?" "How many lines go to Daly City?" Then read the passage aloud while students follow Sue's route with a pencil. Have students erase their markings and then repeat the exercise in pairs, with one student reading while the other traces the route.

B Students answer this with their partners.

2   PRACTICE

A–E Work through these quickly, making sure each stu-

dent understands the task and the correct responses. Call on individual students to read the instructions and provide the correct answers.

F Discuss the symbols. Which of the symbols introduced here have students seen before? Can students guess the meanings without looking at the descriptors? Have students proceed in pairs, doing the exercises first orally, then in writing. Have students put correct answers on the board.

3   REVIEW

A Talk about riding buses. Ask students about bus systems they have used or are using. If possible, bring in examples of bus timetables to discuss as a class. Go over the bus timetable in the text, making sure students understand terms, abbreviations, and how to read the times. Model the example questions, encouraging students to *scan* the timetable quickly, looking for the right information. Then divide the class into two groups. Each group writes five questions and answers about the bus timetable. Then the groups take turns asking each other their questions.

B First have students cover the symbols and guess the meaning of each one. Then let the students match the symbols with their definitions.

Unit 5   Notices

SKILLS COVERED

- Scanning – reading up, down, and across for recognition of text type and purpose.

- Using key words to distinguish relevant information from irrelevant information.

- Applying these skills to directories, notices, lists, and advertisements.

1   READING

- Before reading, predict Machiko's first steps when she gets to college. Ask the students what they did on their first day at their college. How did they feel? Who did they meet? Ask students to identify the location of bulletin boards with information notices and directories in your school.

- If possible, prerecord the dialogue and have students follow along, referring to the registration directory. Then assign roles and have students read the dialogue aloud.

2   PRACTICE

A–B Do these exercises with the class.

C–E These exercises direct students back to the registration directory. Point out that there is more information in the directory than the students need, so they should look only for the relevant information, skipping the items they don't need.

F Ask individual students to read the notice aloud. Then answer the questions as a class.

G Ask students if they have ever looked for a job by reading newspaper advertisements. Bring in examples of "Help Wanted" ads from local newspapers for students to look at and discuss. Go over common abbreviations ("temp.," "F/T or P/T," "tel.," etc.) and common expressions and terms ("apply in writing," "full-time," "part-time," "overtime available," etc.). Do the example in Practice G with the class. Then let the students complete the rest of the items individually or in pairs. Encourage them to work as rapidly as possible, scanning the ads for the relevant information.

H This would be a good homework exercise.

3 REVIEW

A Introduce the hospital directory and go over pronunciation of room names. Do the example questions together, then divide students into pairs and give them about 5 minutes to ask and answer five different questions. Choose couples to read their question-answer sets aloud or write them on the board.

B Familiarize students with the schedule of airline departures. Then read the questions, calling on individual students for answers. Always ask students to explain where and how they found their answers.

READING REVIEW ONE

1 MATCHING PAIRS

First have students complete this individually – in class or as homework. Then have them check answers in small groups. Go over remaining problems with the whole class. The answers are:

A5	F13	K14	P12
B10	G9	L2	Q9
C11	H1	M6	
D8	I3	N4	
E7	J15	O16	

2 PUZZLES

A Divide students into small groups and have them work as teams to complete this exercise as quickly as possible. Have groups give their answers orally to the whole class.

B Continue working in teams for the crossword puzzle. Offer a prize to the team that completes it first.

PART TWO: Reading for Meaning

Unit 1   Instructions

SKILLS COVERED

- Reading, understanding, and carrying out instructions on forms.

- Distinguishing between information questions and choice questions.

- Transferring, tabulating, and evaluating information according to written instructions.

1 READING

- Bring examples of various forms (enrollment, employment, insurance, etc.) to class. Discuss with students what kinds of information are requested on forms and what kinds of instructions commonly appear. Ask students about their experiences with forms, and whether they had to complete them in their native language or in English.

- Go over Machiko's enrollment form with the class. Find examples of (1) instructions about *how* to fill out the form (e.g., "please print" or "check the appropriate box"); (2) information questions (e.g., "name" or "address"); and (3) choice questions (yes/no questions or multiple choice). Ask students if Machiko filled in the information at the bottom of the form. (No.) Why didn't she?

2   PRACTICE

A First have students scan the enrollment form, finding examples of instructions, information questions, and choice questions. Have students work with a partner. Each student completes the form for his or her partner by eliciting all necessary information.

B Have students quickly scan the reservation form. Point out two common abbreviations: No. (number) and N.B. (note well). Explain any vocabulary that is unfamiliar to the students. Then ask questions: "What kind of form is this?" "Who filled it out?" "Where is he going on vacation?" "Who is going with him?" "What is the total cost of the vacation?"

C Have students work alone or in pairs. Check answers orally, asking students *where* they found their answers.

D Make at least two copies of the reservation form for each student, using the blank form at the end of the Teacher's Notes on page 123. Students complete the forms alone or in pairs. Students who work more quickly could complete a third form for themselves or a partner. Collect the forms and duplicate or display correct versions.

3   REVIEW

A (*Note*: To save time, make three to six copies of the questionnaire for each student before class.) Go over the questionnaire with the students until you are sure they can handle it with ease. Then have them complete it alone or as homework.

B This exercise can be handled as a class activity or as homework. Ask students to get the forms completed and then answer the questions in writing.

C Have students present the results of their surveys in brief oral presentations.

Unit 2   Messages

SKILLS COVERED

- Recognizing and interpreting the use of abbreviations as a convention in note-taking, in formal and informal situations.

- Using context and situation to guess the meaning of abbreviated language.

- Converting informal notes to formal messages by giving full lexical value to abbreviated words and by giving full structural value to abbreviated sentences.

1   READING

- Begin by establishing the context of the dialogue: Machiko is leaving a message for Sue at work.

- If you have prerecorded the dialogue, play it for the students while their books are closed. Have them listen for the facts of Machiko's message and jot down notes as the dialogue plays. Repeat this until students have a complete set of notes.

- Have students open their books and listen to the dialogue as they read it. Or, if you have no tape of the dialogue, have students read it aloud.

- Finally, have students compare their notes in small groups. Ask about note-taking methods. Did any students use abbreviations?

2   PRACTICE

A–C These exercises refer back to the dialogue. Before students tackle them, explain the difference between *formal* and *informal*. Ask students why the operator made two versions of the message in Practice B. Which version is more comprehensible? Which would be faster to write? Have students compare their informal notes to the operator's. Students can do Practices A – C in class or as homework.

D–G To do these exercises, students must use clues from the situation and context to guess meaning. Have students complete the questions on their own. Then ask individual students to volunteer answers and to explain how they arrived at their answers.

3   REVIEW

A Have students refer to their own dictionaries, comparing entries for the word "message." Look at other dictionary entries. Have the students complete the exercise in pairs. Check their answers when they are finished.

B Put the message on the chalkboard. Ask students for abbreviations for the words listed in the exercise. Erase those words and substitute their abbreviations.

C Introduce this exercise by discussing the use of telegrams and similar forms of communication. Have any students ever sent or received a telegram? Why is abbreviated language important on telegrams? Assign the exercise as homework.

Unit 3   Facts

SKILLS COVERED

- Identifying the subject and purpose of publicly displayed material (posters, notices).

- Recognizing and extracting important factual information.

- Understanding the following functions: requests, announcements, advertisements, and warnings.

- Practicing some common exercise types, such as true/false and prediction, in guided conversation.

1 READING

Bring in examples of posters and notices. Discuss the content and purpose of each. Ask students about the main bulletin (or information) board in your school. What types of information are posted there? Who posts the information? What methods are used to display or present the information (e.g., posters, handwritten notices)?

2 PRACTICE

A Have students scan the whole bulletin board for typographical features. Then discuss how these features can be used to quickly identify the nature and topic of a poster or notice.

B Ask students to skim the bulletin board to extract facts about time, place, and cost.

C This exercise will help students identify purpose or function. Answer the questions together as a class or have the students work in small groups and share their findings with the whole class.

D Go over one or two items in this exercise with the class, modeling correct responses. Then have students complete the task alone or in pairs.

E Have students complete this exercise in small groups. Give them about 10 minutes. Put the correct answers on the board.

F Students read the poster and the notice silently. Then have them answer the questions orally. Ask additional questions, until the class has thoroughly discussed the contents of both the poster and the notice.

G Students first complete the conversation in pairs. Then have several pairs perform their conversations aloud.

3 REVIEW

Have students bring in markers, paints, glue, poster board, and pictures for their posters. Divide the class into groups of four or five and have each group plan their poster before actually making it. Encourage all students to participate.

Unit 4 Opinions

SKILLS COVERED

- Understanding various types of readings that express opinion.

- Recognizing linguistic forms that express these functions: liking/disliking; agreeing/disagreeing; expressing a favorable/an unfavorable opinion; giving reasons for an opinion.

1 READING

- Have students look át the photos and give their own opinions of the artwork.

- Choose students to read the dialogue aloud, using appropriate intonation. Explain any difficult vocabulary. If students need more work, have them practice the dialogue in small groups.

2 PRACTICE

A–C Working as a class, discuss the meaning of a "good" (favorable) opinion and a "bad" (unfavorable) opinion. Then find examples of each in the dialogue.

D–E Have students complete these exercises in pairs. Check answers orally, asking various pairs to perform their dialogues aloud.

F Students should practice their conversations with their partners. Then ask for volunteers to perform their conversations for the class.

G Have students look at the magazine opinion page. Ask them what it is and what the letters are about. Introduce the topic of television violence by asking students for examples of current television programs that depict violence. What are their opinions on these programs and on the effects of TV violence? Then have the students read the editor's letters to the readers.

H–K Read the letters to the editor aloud while students read silently, or ask one or two students to read them aloud. The exercises invite students to guess reasons. Students work in small groups to complete the exercises. They should use evidence from the letters to support their answers.

3 REVIEW

A–B Introduce this activity with a brief discussion about space exploration: the costs, the benefits, the disadvantages, and so forth. Have students read the letters, looking for key words that will reveal each writer's opinion.

C Ask students to look at the six words listed in the exercise and to classify them into two categories: favorable and unfavorable. Then have students complete the exercise alone. Have a few students write their sentences on the board.

Unit 5   Persuasion

SKILLS COVERED

- Understanding various types of readings that use the language of persuasion.

- Recognizing the use of repetition, alliteration, and exaggeration.

- Recognizing the use of word groups that refer to the same subject, have the same sound, and the same favorable connotation.

- Identifying the relationship between form and function in questions, suggestions, and instructions.

1   READING

- Have students look at the photos and guess what is going to happen.

- Discuss the menu with the students. Ask questions such as "Would you like to eat there?" and "What would you order?" Explain any difficult vocabulary. Bring other examples of menus to class to discuss.

- Model the dialogue, using the appropriate intonation. (Or prerecord the dialogue and play it for the class.) Explain any difficult vocabulary. Then choose three students to read the dialogue aloud.

2   PRACTICE

A–C Students work in pairs or small groups, at a pace appropriate to their level. Check answers orally.

D Do this exercise as a class. Point out that the structure of a sentence may not be the same as the meaning of the sentence. (For example, "Why not try our fresh fruit salad?" is structured as a question, but has the effect of a persuasive suggestion.)

E Introduce this exercise by asking students to bring printed advertisements to class. Identify examples of persuasive language in the ads. Next, have students quickly skim the Toshiba cooktop ad, identifying as quickly as possible what the ad is for. Then have them read the ad and answer the questions.

F–G Have students complete this exercise independently, if possible. Explain that they do not need to know all the vocabulary to answer the questions. Give help when needed.

3   REVIEW

A Prepare for this activity by bringing markers and poster board to class. You may want to do a sample advertisement with the class before having them start on their own. Brainstorm for products and appropriate language, writing students' ideas on the board. Then choose one idea and develop it into an advertisement. Proceed by putting students into small groups to work on their own advertisements. Have students take turns presenting their ads to the class.

B Review Machiko's complaints about the restaurant. Look back at Roberto's letter in the first unit to review business letter format. Then have students work alone writing the letters. Have some of the stronger students read their letters aloud to the class.

READING REVIEW TWO

Have students read the story and complete the exercises individually, in class, or as homework. Then have them check their answers in small groups, and go over any questions or problems with the whole class. Finally, have them retell the story in their own words.

For the last exercise (3B – "Putting Events in Order"), you may wish to let your students choose between the written and oral assignments, encouraging the more fluent or confident students to attempt the oral retelling. Have students who chose the written assignment exchange papers with a partner, who adds any facts or information that had not been included.

PART THREE: Reading for Pleasure

Unit 1 Comic Strips and Cartoons

SKILLS COVERED

- Using the content and style of illustrations as clues to context and meaning.

- Practicing questions of fact and questions of inference.

- Answering multiple-choice questions.

1   READING

- Discuss comic strips and cartoons with the class. Ask who reads them in their native countries/cultures – adults, children, or both. If possible, bring examples of comics and cartoons from other countries and cultures to class.

- Read the introductory paragraph with the students and explain the vocabulary.

- Have the students scan the *Mallet* comic strip by themselves.

2 PRACTICE

A Have students work individually. Check answers orally.

B Students will have to infer or deduce their answers. Have them work individually. When checking answers orally, ask students *how* they arrived at their answers.

C Remind students about the differences between *thought* and *speech* bubbles. Have them scan the comic strip silently to get the gist of the storyline. Then have them complete the exercise.

D Make sure students understand what a *warning*, a *question*, and an *apology* are before they begin. Have them work in small groups or pairs. Then have some students read their bubbles aloud to the class.

3 REVIEW

A–D Go over the directions for the exercises, making sure the students understand. Then have students complete the exercises, working in pairs or small groups. Check answers orally. If you and/or students brought examples of comic strips and cartoons to class, have students ask and answer similar questions about them.

Unit 2   Magazines

SKILLS COVERED

- Identifying the functions and linguistic forms characteristic of biographical writing.

- Using reference skills to extract facts.

- Differentiating between fact and opinion.

- Practicing true/false and completion exercises.

1 READING

- Introduce the unit topic by asking students what magazines they read. Ask them if they ever read rock music magazines or magazines with articles about the lives of famous people (e.g., *Rolling Stone* or *People*).

- Read the storyline paragraph with them.

- Have students look at the page from the rock magazine. It is not necessary for them to read the entire selection. Instead, they should scan it, looking at the photos, the headings, and the rock group members' names.

2 PRACTICE

A Discuss the examples about Mike Donovan with the class. Point out the categories (events, facts, etc.) and show how they work as clues to guide the reader to the correct information in the biography. Have students identify where each piece of information is located in the biography.

B–E These exercises require students to use headings in the text for quick reference work and then to use the information they have extracted to answer completion exercises and true/false questions. Have students work in pairs or small groups and then present their answers orally to the class.

F Introduce this exercise by eliciting facts the students may already know about Elvis Presley. Then ask them to scan the article, looking at the title, photos, and first sentences of each paragraph. Finally, have them read the article silently, asking any questions they have about vocabulary or meaning.

G Students should be able to complete this exercise on their own. As an aid, write the numbers 1 through 8 on the board and then ask students which event would be first (Elvis was born) and which would be last (Elvis died).

H Go over the words and phrases about time, modeling their use. Have students complete the exercise alone. Then ask some students to read their paragraphs aloud.

I Review the differences between fact and opinion, discussing one or two examples. (For example: "Elvis made many films" is a *fact*; "Elvis made too many films" is an *opinion*.) Have students complete the exercise alone or in pairs.

J This task focuses on a very important discourse feature: pronoun reference. Go over the example with the students. Put a list of pronouns on the board. Then guide the students through the exercise.

3 REVIEW

First, read the directions aloud, explaining them if necessary. Have students look at the outline while you read the jumbled paragraph aloud. Be sure to pause between sentences. Students can work in small groups or pairs to complete the outline. They should write the correct paragraph individually.

Unit 3   Nonfiction

SKILLS COVERED

- Using textual and extra-textual clues to predict words or meaning.

- Using word groups and context to predict words or meaning.

- Applying the preceding skills to multiple-choice and completion exercises.

1 READING

- Prepare for this unit in advance by bringing a few non-fiction books (e.g., guide books, how-to books) to class and by asking students to bring their English-English dictionaries. Briefly discuss with the students how and why they might use one of the books you have brought to class. Ask what they would look for first; then ask where they would find that information in the book.

- Read the storyline paragraph with the class. Explain the vocabulary, asking students to scan the unit and find an example of each vocabulary item.

2 PRACTICE

A Have students work in pairs. They should first guess the missing words, using only the context. Then they should check their guesses against the clues. Finally, they should check their answers with their dictionaries.

B Students must refer to the contents page of *This Is New York* to do this exercise. Point out that each sentence contains a key word that acts as a clue. (For example, the date *1626* in item 1 suggests that the excerpt is from the chapter on history.) Have students complete the task alone. Then check answers orally, asking students what word or words acted as clues.

C This task focuses on several brief excerpts from *This Is New York*. First read the excerpts aloud, explaining any new vocabulary. Go over the example, pointing out that the first answer is taken directly from the excerpt, but that the second answer is inferred. Then read the incomplete dialogue aloud, while students follow in their books. Finally, have the students complete the task in pairs. Assign roles and have a few of the stronger students read the completed dialogue aloud.

D Do the first few items with the class. Then have the students complete the rest on their own. Check answers orally.

3 REVIEW

A First, ask students what they do for entertainment. Write their responses on the board. Then compare the students' list with the items in the Review example. Go over the instructions and explain any new vocabulary. Then have students complete the exercises in pairs or small groups.

B Check students' answers to the exercises in A orally. Then do B as a class.

Unit 4   Fiction

SKILLS COVERED

- Making predictions before reading.

- Taking notes while reading.

- Summarizing and evaluating after reading.

- Practicing study skills for note-taking, describing, comparing, and recording.

1 READING

- Read the storyline paragraph with the class and answer the prediction question about the book *The House on the Hill*.

- Read Chapter 1 aloud while students read silently.

2 PRACTICE

A Have students read Chapter 1 again, this time taking notes in the spaces provided in the outline. Go over the completed outlines orally.

B Have students write the paragraphs individually. (This could be assigned as homework.) Ask a few of the stronger students to write their paragraphs on the board.

C First go over the background information with the class. Then have students read the second excerpt silently.

D Read the instructions aloud, explaining the differences between "least likely," "possible," and "most likely." Have the students complete the task in small groups. Then have each group present their answers and explain the reasons for their answers.

3 READING

- Read the storyline information with the class, making sure the students understand the terms (especially "simplified edition").

- Have students read the introductory remarks about *Hotel*. Put a list of the characters on the board and elicit from the students an identifying phrase about each.

- Read Texts A and B aloud, while students follow silently. Then have students read the two texts again on their own.

4 PRACTICE

A Students can complete this task alone. Check answers orally, asking students *where* they found their answers.

B Do this exercise as a class. Students may wish to add some of the words to their vocabulary lists.

5 REVIEW

Ask students to share information about books they have read before they begin writing their summaries. The summaries can be done in class or for homework. Have students present their summaries orally in class.

Unit 5   A Theater Visit

SKILLS COVERED

- Reviewing the reasons and strategies for reading for information, meaning, and pleasure.

- Reviewing a variety of text types and features relevant to the topic.

- Reviewing and practicing yes/no, true/false, cloze, scanning for information, and multiple-choice exercise types.

1 READING

- Remind students of the storyline of the book. Machiko and Roberto are meeting Sue and Peter at the theater.

- Have students read the introductory paragraph and scan the opening pages of the unit to find an excerpt about (a) the theater, (b) the play, (c) the author, (d) the actors, and (e) where to eat after the show.

- Now have students read each of the excerpts carefully.

2 PRACTICE

A–E Have students complete the exercises in this Practice alone or in pairs. Check answers orally, asking students *where* they found the correct information.

3 REVIEW

Read the storyline information with the class. Have students scan the Review section and identify the various text types. Answer questions and go over difficult vocabulary.

A–C In these exercises, students find the information in the short texts to complete the dialogues. Have the students work in pairs or small groups. Check answers orally, and have students explain where they found their answers.

READING REVIEW THREE

1   WHAT PEOPLE READ

A Have students look at the photos of the people and the magazines. Ask them to predict what kind of readers (age, income, sex, interests, etc.) would buy each magazine.

B Guide students through this exercise example. On the board list the four categories (gender, age group, home, and income group). Under each heading, list words or phrases used to describe that category. (For instance, under "Home," list words like "city," "suburb," "country," and "rural.")

C Have students complete the paragraphs for the rest of the magazines individually, in class or as homework.

2   WHY PEOPLE READ

A–B Read through the background information and the chart with the students. Make sure they can use the information.

C–F Have students complete these exercises individually, in class or as homework.

RESERVATION FORM

Part Two, Unit 1   Instructions, 2   Practice, D, page 37.

 **Euro Tours Inc.**
Reservation Form

PLEASE PRINT

Name _____

              Last   First   Middle Initial

Address _____

Phone Number _____

Cities		Persons	No.	Rooms		
Which will you visit?						
City	**No. of nights**	Adults		**Type**	**No.**	**Bath** (CIRCLE)
Amsterdam				Single		YES NO
Athens		Children				
Florence		(3 - 14 yrs)		Twin		YES NO
London				(1 rm. 2 beds)		
Madrid		Infants				
Munich		(under 3 yrs)		Double		YES NO
Paris				(1 rm. 1 bed)		
Rome						
Venice				Triple		YES NO
Zurich				(1 rm. 3 beds)		

YOUR ACCOMMODATION COSTS			CHARGES (accommodation only)	
Per night:	Adult(s)		Each adult	: $30 per night
	Child(ren)		Each child	: $20 per night
	Bathroom(s)		Each bathroom	: $10 per night
Total per night			Infants	: FREE
Total no. of nights			N.B. Fares are separate	

TOTAL ACCOMMODATION COST		

I enclose a deposit of _____   SIGNED _____

Acknowledgments

The authors and publisher thank the following for the use of their material and for providing illustrations:

Lynne Hale, for photographs on the cover and on pp. 2, 3, 7, 12, 24, 30, 40, 47, 52 (bottom left), 53, 58, 59, 70 (top right), 75, and 96.

p. 17, the Fine Arts Museums of San Francisco for permission to use the floor plan of the M. H. de Young Memorial Museum.

p. 19, the Bay Area Rapid Transit District for permission to use their BART map.

p. 22, the San Francisco Visitors Information Bureau for the bus schedule.

p. 52 (top), photo by Kenneth C. Poertner.

p. 52 (bottom right), © 1980 Michael Lichter Photography.

p. 55 (left), © 1989 Karelle Scharff, Private Eye Photography.

p. 61, created by Calet, Hirsch & Spector, Inc. for Toshiba America, Inc.

pp. 65–66, illustrations by Tony Morris.

pp. 70–71, illustrations by Leslie Branton.

pp. 72 and 73 (top) illustrations by Stephen De Stefano.

p. 73 (center), *Young Romance*, Vol. 24, No. 202, Dec. 1974, p. 92. *Young Romance* is a trademark of DC Comics Inc. Illustration: © 1974 DC Comics Inc. All rights reserved. Used With Permission.

p. 73 (bottom), cartoon by Jim Borgman, reprinted with special permission of King Features Syndicate, Inc.

p. 74 (top), illustration by Stephen De Stefano.

p. 74 (margin), illustration from *Star Lord*. *Star Lord* is a trademark of Marvel Entertainment Group, Inc. and is used with permission. Copyright © 1990, Marvel Entertainment Group, Inc. All rights reserved.

p. 75 (bottom), photograph by Marc P. Anderson.

p. 76, photographs by Marc P. Anderson.

p. 78, photographs of Elvis Presley courtesy of UPI/Bettmann.

pp. 81–83, 85, Heinemann Educational Books Ltd. and the author for permission to use extracts from *This is New York* by Betsy Pennink.

p. 85 (top), photo courtesy of the New York Convention and Visitor's Bureau.

p. 85 (center), photo courtesy of the New York State Department of Commerce.

p. 85 (bottom), © Ulf Sjostedt/FPG International.

p. 88, illustration by Stephen De Stefano.

pp. 89, 91, Heinemann Educational Books Ltd. and the author for permission to use extracts from *The House on the Hill* by Elizabeth Laird. Published in Heinemann Guided Readers Series, 1978.

pp. 92, 93, excerpts from *Hotel* by Arthur Hailey, copyright © 1965 by Arthur Hailey, Ltd. Used by permission of Doubleday, a division of Bantam, Doubleday, Dell Publishing Group, Inc., U.S.A., and Souvenir Press, Ltd., England.

p. 100, photograph by Wide World Photos, Inc.

p. 101, from *Death of a Salesman* by Arthur Miller. Copyright 1949, renewed © 1977 by Arthur Miller. All rights reserved. Reprinted by permission of Viking Penguin, a division of Penguin Books USA, Inc., and International Creative Management, Inc.

p. 103 (top left), © Cleo Freelance Photo.

p. 103 (top right), *Jack and Jill* cover used by permission of Children's Better Health & Medical Society, Indianapolis, IN.

p. 103 (bottom left), © James G. White Photography.

p. 104 (top left), photo © Ron Chapple/FPG International.

p. 104 (center right), photo © Paul O. Boisvert/FPG International.

p. 104 (bottom left), photo © Cheryl A. Ertelt.

p. 106 (top left), photo by Skjold Photographers.

p. 106, *Birth of Fire* and *Exit Earth*, courtesy of Baen Books.

p. 106 (center right), © 1986 Mike Valeri/FPG International.

p. 106 (bottom left), © Jeffry W. Myers/FPG International.

p. 107 (top left), photo by Marc P. Anderson.

p. 107, map reprinted from *Shaker Village Views: Illustrated Maps and Landscape Drawings by Shaker Artists of the Nineteenth Century*, by Robert P. Emlen, University Press of New England, Hanover, NH, © 1987 Robert P. Emlen.

p. 107 (top right), photo by Sandra Graham.

Every effort has been made to trace the owners of copyright material in this book. We would be grateful to hear from anyone who recognizes their copyright material and who is unacknowledged. We will be pleased to make the necessary corrections in future editions of the book.